NOTEWORTHY RETURNS

The Quiet Power of Investing in Real Estate Notes

by Dave Storton

Professional Testimonials

"Thanks to DSRT Property Solutions, I was able to achieve my financial goals much faster than I thought possible. Dave Storton's expertise and integrity are unmatched. He has been very helpful and responsive to all of my questions throughout the process. I have been using his services for several years, and I will continue to do so in the foreseeable future."
— **Ron W.**

"Dave continuously studies the market to make certain that those who invest with him are well taken care of. Dave is always open to discussing the current condition of my account and makes sure that I am aware of new opportunities. My account is well-managed, and the distributions are always on time. I have full confidence in Dave's ability to manage my account and to provide me with an outstanding return on investment."
— **Ed F.**

"We have chosen to invest with Dave due primarily to his integrity and credibility, as well as his proven performance in this field. His experience both as an investor and as a former investigator has proven to be top-notch. We feel very comfortable and confident in entrusting our funds to Dave for safe, legal, and financially beneficial growth."
— **Lloyd O.**

"When Dave started ...DSRT Property Solutions... his enthusiasm was elevated once again, and he took the time to explain to me how the company would work. I was very impressed with the company plan and decided to invest in it. Dave provides regular updates on the company, and I feel very confident in his management abilities as this company grows..."
— **J.R.**

"In 2021, I invested with Dave and have had no regrets in doing so. My financial portfolio has increased as promised ever since. Dave is a very straightforward person who can explain his financial strategies clearly and in a way that provides comfort and clear direction for my future.
Dave is a rare personality in my mind as he is one of the most consistent, down-to-earth people I've ever met, and he has proven this to me since 1993."
— **Dave B.**

"I have known Dave Storton for several decades. He was a well-respected and hard-working colleague during my years in law enforcement. I have also had the pleasure of investing in a property acquisition company he co-managed. One of the many things that prompted me to invest in Dave's company was his impeccable reputation, tireless work ethic, money-wise acumen, and desire to encourage and lift people up and help them succeed in their life endeavors and financial situations." — **David S.**

"In the investment world where scams, greed, and dishonesty are so pervasive, I found the fact that Dave chose to only deal with friends and associates from a rather narrow professional field to be refreshingly transparent, and a strategy that further solidified that he was uniquely trustworthy." — **Client**

"I had a very successful experience with Dave's company and would not hesitate to recommend it as a wise addition to an investment portfolio." — **Client**

"When I learned that Dave was providing investment opportunities, I reached out to him. Dave's expertise was obvious as he explained his investment strategies to me in a direct and easy to understand way. He was a patient teacher who sincerely wanted me to learn his ideas, and if I chose, he would help me implement them...I feel I am very fortunate for the opportunity to invest with him. Thanks to Dave I have been making money from the first day of my investment and every day since." — **Robert M.**

"Through all of my interactions with Dave, I can assure you he is extremely professional, detail oriented, and a conscientious human being. He scours for the best investment deals, and I have found his investments to be rock solid! Last but not least, when investing with Dave, he makes sure you understand all that is involved and makes deploying your money a simple and smooth process!" — **Jeff W.**

"Because of Dave's knowledge, judgment, and work ethic, I have invested with him and have been very successful. I would recommend Dave to anyone interested in investment opportunities." — **Randy J.**

Acknowledgments

I would like to express my gratitude to Eddie Speed, Joe Varnadore, and Kevin Moore who launched me on my note investing journey and who continue to mentor me to this day.

Edition V.1 2024

ISBN Paperback: 979-8-9909566-2-9
ISBN E-book: 979-8-9909566-3-6

Publisher:
DSRT Property Solutions, LLC and Book Done for You
Cover Design, Formatting, Editing:
bookdoneforyou.com

Table of Contents

Introduction

Over 70% of Americans are unprepared for retirement. This stark and unsettling statistic underscores a pervasive crisis in personal financial management. Yet, within this crisis lies a less-trodden path to financial security, which has quietly outperformed traditional investment avenues for those in the know. This path is the investment in real estate notes.

Noteworthy Returns: The Quiet Power of Investing in Real Estate Notes unveils this often-overlooked vehicle of wealth accumulation and cash flow. This book will provide a launching pad for the real estate note investing world. The information contained herein will give passive note investors who wish to partner with an active expert in pursuit of passive returns a good understanding of notes and how these paper assets, backed by real estate, can provide consistent and secure returns.

For those who wish to wade into deeper waters by sourcing and originating their notes, *Noteworthy Returns* will provide a solid foundation for becoming a more active, hands-on investor. It will also demystify the process of investing in real estate notes.

Real estate notes, or mortgage notes, offer a unique blend of stability, predictable cash flow, and the potential for significant returns, all while mitigating many of the risks associated with direct property ownership.

Throughout the pages of *Noteworthy Returns*, I will guide you through the intricacies of note investing, from understanding the basics to developing strategies to safeguarding your retirement.

Prepare to embark on a journey that could redefine your approach to financial planning. Leverage the quiet power of real estate notes for noteworthy returns...

As we delve deeper, we will explore the historical performance of real estate notes compared to traditional investments. We'll also explore the mechanisms that make them a stable yet lucrative option. And finally, we'll explore how to navigate the market to find opportunities that align with your financial goals.

Whether navigating your career, approaching retirement, or enjoying your golden years, this book will help you harness the power of real estate notes to build and protect your wealth, plan for retirement, and/or cash flow your savings for supplemental income.

Noteworthy Returns will arm you with the knowledge and strategies I've honed over years of successful investing and working with the foremost experts in the note investing space. From deciphering the legal landscape to mastering the art of risk assessment and beyond, we'll cover the A to Z of real estate note investment. Moreover, I will share personal anecdotes and case studies that illustrate both the pitfalls to avoid and the paths to success.

With this book as your guide, real estate note investing will no longer be an intimidating mystery but a clear opportunity for securing a prosperous future. *Noteworthy Returns* will illuminate a path to financial security for you *and* inspire you to take the steps necessary to achieve it.

— **Dave Storton**

DSRT Property Solutions, LLC
Contact Dave:
Dave@DSRT.us
www.dsrt.us

CHAPTER 1

Unlocking the Vault: The Basics of Real Estate Notes

What are Real Estate Notes?

Understanding the specific terms and concepts related to real estate notes is not just a matter of academic interest; it's a prerequisite for anyone looking to confidently and efficiently navigate the complex waters of mortgage lending and investment portfolios. This essential knowledge is critically important! It serves as the bedrock upon which the forthcoming discourse is built, guiding us through the intricacies of real estate investment and the pivotal role that notes play. As we delve into this section, we will explore a concise list of terms, including 'Mortgage Note,' 'Promissory Note,' 'Deed of Trust,' and 'Lien.' These terms will serve as beacons, illuminating our path through the complex landscape of real estate investing.

Mortgage Note:

A Mortgage Note, often referred to simply as a "note," is a legally binding agreement between a borrower and a lender that outlines the terms and conditions of a loan used to finance the purchase of a property. It serves as the cornerstone of the mortgage process, embodying the financial commitment and obligations of both parties involved.

Critical Components of a Mortgage Note:

Identification of Parties:

The mortgage note begins by identifying the parties involved in the transaction: the borrower (the mortgagor) and the lender (also known as the mortgagee). Their legal names typically identify each party and may include additional information such as addresses and contact details.

Loan Amount and Terms:

The note specifies the principal amount of the loan, which represents the total amount borrowed by the borrower. It outlines the loan terms, including the interest rate charged on the principal amount, the type of interest (fixed or adjustable), and the repayment schedule (e.g., monthly or bi-weekly).

Repayment Terms:

One of the most critical aspects of the mortgage note is the repayment term, which details how the borrower will repay the loan. This term includes the installment payment amount, the due date for each payment, and any penalties or fees for late payments. The note may also outline options for prepayment or early loan payoff.

Security Instrument:

In addition to the mortgage note, the borrower typically signs a separate document known as a mortgage or Deed of Trust. This document serves as a security instrument, providing the lender with a legal interest in the property as collateral for the loan. In default, the lender may foreclose on the property to satisfy the debt.

Default and Remedies:

The mortgage note also specifies the consequences of default, outlining the actions that the lender may take if the borrower fails to make timely payments. Such actions may include late fees, foreclosure proceedings, and potential property loss. Borrowers must understand their obligations and the repercussions of default outlined in the note.

Significance of the Mortgage Note:

The mortgage note is pivotal in real estate transactions, providing clarity, transparency, and legal enforceability to the lending and borrowing process. It is a tangible representation of the borrower's commitment to repay the loan and the lender's right to receive payment according to the agreed-upon terms.

Importance of Understanding the Mortgage Note:

Understanding the terms and conditions outlined in the mortgage note is essential for borrowers to make informed financial decisions and ensure compliance with the loan agreement. It empowers borrowers to manage their finances responsibly and avoid pitfalls like default and foreclosure.

Similarly, the mortgage note serves as a legal safeguard for lenders, providing recourse in the event of borrower default and protecting their financial interests. By clearly defining the terms of the loan and the rights and obligations of both parties, the note helps mitigate risks and ensure a smooth and transparent lending process.

The mortgage note is a fundamental document in the mortgage process, embodying the financial agreement between the borrower and the lender.

Promissory Note:

While closely related to the Mortgage Note, the Promissory Note is its broader counterpart, serving as a foundational document in financial transactions. It is a legally binding financial instrument that evidences a promise made by one party (the borrower) to pay a specific sum of money to another party (the lender) at a specified time or on demand.

Key Components of a Promissory Note:

Identification of Parties:

Like the Mortgage Note, the Promissory Note begins by identifying the parties involved in the transaction: the borrower (also known as the maker) and the lender (also known as the payee). Their legal names typically identify each party and may include additional information such as addresses and contact details.

Promise to Pay:

At its core, the Promissory Note contains a promise by the borrower to repay the borrowed amount to the lender according to specified terms. This promise includes the principal amount borrowed, any accrued interest, and any additional fees or charges associated with the loan.

Terms of Repayment:

The note outlines the repayment terms, including the repayment schedule, interest rate, and any applicable fees or penalties for late payments. It may specify whether the loan will be repaid in installments or as a lump sum and the frequency of payments (e.g., monthly or quarterly).

Interest Rate and Calculation Method:

The Promissory Note specifies the interest rate charged on the loan and how it is calculated. This may include whether it is fixed or variable, the annual percentage rate (APR), and any conditions or adjustments that may affect the rate over time.

Maturity Date:

The note includes the maturity date and the date the borrower is required to repay the loan in full. Sometimes, the note also allows for early repayment or prepayment of the loan without penalty.

Default and Remedies:

Like the Mortgage Note, the Promissory Note outlines the consequences of default, including late fees, penalties, and the lender's rights to pursue legal remedies such as foreclosure or repossession of collateral.

Significance of the Promissory Note:

The Promissory Note is a critical document in financial transactions. It is tangible evidence of the borrower's obligation to repay the loan and the lender's right to receive payment according to the agreed-upon terms. It provides legal clarity and enforceability to the lending and borrowing process, ensuring accountability and protecting the interests of both parties involved.

Role of the Promissory Note in Real Estate Notes:

In the context of real estate notes, the Promissory Note often accompanies a Mortgage Note or Deed of Trust, which serves as a security instrument providing the lender with a legal interest in the property as collateral for the loan. Together, these documents form the basis of the borrower-lender relationship in real estate financing, outlining the terms and conditions of the loan and the rights and obligations of each party.

The Promissory Note is a fundamental component of financial transactions, including real estate notes. It serves as a testament to the borrower's commitment to repay the loan and the lender's right to receive payment. Understanding its key components and significance is essential for all parties involved in lending and borrowing, empowering them to navigate the complexities of financial transactions with confidence and clarity.

Understanding the Promissory Note and Mortgage Note: A Comparison

While closely related, Promissory and Mortgage Notes serve distinct but interconnected roles in financial transactions, particularly in real estate financing. Let's delve into the nuances of each and explore how they compare and contrast:

Key Differences:

Scope of Application:

The Promissory Note extends beyond real estate transactions. It applies to various borrowing and lending scenarios, including personal loans, business loans, and financing agreements. In contrast, the Mortgage Note is specific to real estate financing and is used to secure loans to purchase or refinance real property.

Legal Enforcement:

Both the Promissory Note and Mortgage Note are legally enforceable documents, but they serve different purposes in terms of enforcement. The Promissory Note primarily governs the borrower's obligation to repay the loan. At the same time, the Mortgage Note establishes the lender's rights to foreclose on the property in the event of default.

Collateralization:

The Promissory Note does not inherently involve collateral. Still, in the realm of real estate, it is typically associated with an Agreement for Deed (Land Contract.) The underlying real estate property secures the Mortgage Note. This security means that in addition to the borrower's guarantee to repay the loan, the lender has recourse to the property as collateral in the event of default.

Key Similarities:

Legal Binding:

The Promissory Note and Mortgage Note are legally binding contracts that establish the terms and conditions of the loan agreement between the borrower and lender.

Financial Obligation:

Both documents embody the borrower's financial obligation to repay the loan according to the agreed-upon terms, including the repayment schedule, interest rate, and other conditions specified in the notes.

Risk Mitigation:

The Promissory and Mortgage Notes serve as risk mitigation tools, providing clarity, transparency, and legal enforceability to the lending and borrowing process.

In summary, while the Promissory and Mortgage Notes share similarities in their role as legally binding agreements governing loan transactions, they also exhibit distinct differences in scope, application, and collateralization. Understanding these nuances is essential for all parties involved in real estate financing, empowering them to navigate the complexities of borrowing and lending with confidence and clarity.

Deed of Trust:

A Deed of Trust is a critical component of real estate lending, serving as a safeguard for both lenders and borrowers in the lending process. Let's explore the intricacies of the Deed of Trust and its significance in real estate transactions:

Critical Elements of a Deed of Trust:

Property Conveyance:

At its core, a Deed of Trust represents an agreement where the borrower, the trustor, conveys the property's title to a designated trustee. This conveyance serves as security for the repayment of the debt owed to the lender, also known as the beneficiary.

Three-Party Agreement:

Unlike a traditional mortgage, which involves two parties (the borrower and lender), a Deed of Trust is a three-party agreement involving the borrower, lender, and trustee. The trustee holds legal title to the property on behalf of the lender until the loan is repaid or the property is foreclosed.

Collateralization of the Loan:

By executing a Deed of Trust, the borrower pledges the property as collateral for the loan, providing the lender with recourse in the event of default. This collateralization mitigates the lender's risk and increases the likelihood of loan approval, often resulting in more favorable loan terms for the borrower.

Significance of the Deed of Trust:

The Deed of Trust is pivotal in real estate lending, ensuring all parties' interests are protected and aligned. Here's why it's essential:

Property Security:

For lenders, the Deed of Trust provides a legal mechanism to secure their interest in the property, reducing the risk of financial loss in the event of borrower default. This security gives lenders confidence to extend credit and offer competitive loan terms to borrowers.

Borrower Protection:

While the Deed of Trust serves as collateral for the loan, it also protects borrowers by establishing clear guidelines for foreclosure proceedings.

Borrowers can cure defaults, negotiate repayment plans, and seek legal recourse if their rights are violated during foreclosure.

Trustee Oversight:

The trustee appointed in the Deed of Trust acts as a neutral third party responsible for holding legal title to the property on behalf of the lender. This impartial oversight ensures transparency and fairness in handling the property's title throughout the life of the loan.

The Deed of Trust is a fundamental component of real estate lending, providing a framework for property collateralization and loan security. Its three-party structure safeguards the borrower, lender, and trustee, ensuring all parties' interests are aligned, fostering trust and confidence in the lending process.

Lien:

A lien is a cornerstone in finance, representing a legal safeguard for creditors to secure the payment of debts or the fulfillment of obligations. A lien is a legal right or claim a creditor acquires against a property. It serves as collateral to ensure the repayment of a debt or the performance of an obligation by the property owner, also known as the debtor. This financial mechanism acts as a safety net, providing creditors with a means of recourse in the event of default.

Let's delve into the intricacies of liens and their significance in the context of real estate notes.

Vital Elements of Liens:

Securing Debts and Obligations:

Liens serve as a mechanism for creditors to secure the debts owed to them by the property owner. Whether it's a mortgage loan, a judgment debt, or a tax obligation, the existence of a lien grants creditors the legal right to stake a claim on the property's value to satisfy the debt.

Priority and Hierarchy:

In the complex web of real estate transactions, liens establish a priority hierarchy, dictating the order in which creditors are entitled to receive payment from the proceeds of a property's sale or foreclosure. Understanding this hierarchy is crucial for determining the extent of a creditor's rights and the potential risks associated with a property.

Notice and Recording:

Liens must typically be recorded or filed with the appropriate government authority to establish validity and enforceability against third parties. This recording process serves as a form of public notice, alerting potential buyers, lenders, and other interested parties to the lien's existence on the property.

Significance of Liens in Real Estate Notes:

Understanding liens is paramount for investors and lenders alike. Here's why:

Layers of Protection:

Liens add layers of protection for lenders by providing a legal interest in the property as collateral. In the event of borrower default, creditors with valid liens can initiate foreclosure proceedings to recoup their losses by selling the property.

Priority Considerations:

Investors must carefully assess the priority of liens when evaluating real estate notes. Senior liens, such as first mortgages, typically take precedence over junior liens, such as second mortgages or judgment liens, in distributing proceeds from a property sale or foreclosure.

Risk Management:

Understanding the presence and implications of liens enables investors to conduct thorough due diligence and assess the potential risks associated with a property or loan investment. By identifying and mitigating lien-related risks, investors can make informed decisions to protect their interests and maximize returns.

Liens play a fundamental role in real estate finance, providing creditors with a legal mechanism to secure their interests in property and ensuring the fulfillment of debts or obligations. For investors and lenders in real estate notes, a comprehensive understanding of liens is essential for navigating the complexities of property transactions and safeguarding their investments.

Agreement for Deed (Land Contract):

As a note investor or asset manager, understanding an Agreement for Deed, commonly known as a land contract, is essential when evaluating potential investments or managing existing ones in your portfolio. By understanding land contracts' differences, risks, and considerations, investors can make informed investment decisions and effectively manage their portfolios to achieve their financial objectives.

Here's how land contracts differ from traditional notes secured by a deed of trust and the considerations for note investors:

Key Differences and Considerations:

Title Ownership and Security Interest:

In a land contract arrangement, the seller retains legal title to the property until the buyer fulfills all contract terms, including payment in full. However, when a note investor acquires the note and land contract, they effectively step into the seller's shoes, assuming legal title to the property or holding a security interest through the entity acquiring the land contract. This transition means that the investor does hold a security interest in the property, similar to traditional notes secured by a deed of trust. As a note investor, it's crucial to understand the legal implications of this transition and ensure that appropriate documentation is in place to protect the investor's interests in the property.

- *Risk and Return Profile:*

Land contracts offer unique risk and return profiles compared to traditional notes secured by a deed of trust. While land contracts may provide opportunities for higher interest rates and the potential for greater returns, they also carry specific risks, such as title issues, tax liabilities, and limited legal protections for investors in the event of borrower default. As a note investor, assessing and weighing these risks against potential returns is crucial when considering land contract investments.

- *Legal Considerations:*

Investors should carefully review the terms of the land contract, including default remedies, provisions for title insurance, and mechanisms for resolving disputes. Understanding the legal framework governing land contracts in the relevant jurisdiction is essential for effectively managing investments and mitigating legal risks. Additionally, investors should know potential regulatory requirements and compliance considerations associated with land contract investments.

Pros and Cons of Land Contracts for Note Investors:

Pros:

- *Higher Interest Rates:*

Land contracts offer investors opportunities to earn higher interest rates than traditional notes secured by a deed of trust, potentially enhancing overall portfolio returns.

- *Portfolio Diversification:*

Land contracts allow investors to diversify their portfolios beyond traditional note investments, potentially reducing overall risk and increasing investment opportunities.

Cons:

- *Title Risk:*

Land contracts expose investors to potential title issues and encumbrances, which could affect the investor's ability to enforce their rights and remedies in the event of borrower default.

- *Tax Liability:*

Investors may be responsible for property taxes and other expenses if the borrower fails to fulfill their obligations under the land contract, increasing the investor's financial exposure and potential losses.

CONCLUSION:

As we reflect on these terms and their definitions, we must recognize their applicability in the abstract and real-world scenarios that investors and borrowers face daily. Each term represents a piece of the real estate investing puzzle, and understanding these pieces is essential for anyone looking to build or manage a successful investment portfolio. These concepts are not isolated islands of knowledge; they are interconnected components of the larger narrative of real estate investment. As we progress through this book, we will explore these terms in greater depth, uncovering their implications, challenges, and opportunities. This foundation will enhance our understanding of real estate notes and equip us with the insights to navigate the broader real estate investing landscape confidently and critically.

CHAPTER 2

The Evolution of Note Investing

N ow that we've laid out the terms and concepts of real estate notes, let's delve deeper into the historical context to better appreciate these instruments' evolution and significance in today's investment landscape.

This historical overview aims to provide a comprehensive understanding of how investing in real estate notes has morphed over time, shedding light on the shifts in practices, regulations, and investor perceptions that have shaped the current market.

The timeline of real estate note investing is rich and varied, spanning several centuries and encompassing numerous economic cycles, legal reforms, and technological advancements. To grasp the magnitude of its evolution, we must start at the very beginning:

- *Early Roots:*

We can trace real estate notes back to ancient civilizations, where records of land sales and agreements were kept on clay tablets and papyrus. However, the modern incarnation of the mortgage note began to take shape in the medieval period in England. Landowners would secure loans against their land, with written agreements detailing the repayment terms. This period laid the groundwork for the legal and financial frameworks that would evolve into today's real estate note investing.

- *19th Century:*

The Industrial Revolution and the expansion of the banking sector brought about significant changes in real estate transactions. The introduction of formalized lending institutions and the standardization of mortgage documents made real estate notes more accessible and reliable as investment vehicles.

- *20th Century:*

The Great Depression of the 1930s led to a pivotal shift in the U.S. government's role in the housing market, with the creation of the Federal Housing Administration (FHA) and the secondary mortgage market. These developments introduced new levels of security and liquidity to real estate note investing, encouraging broader participation.

- *Late 20th to Early 21st Century:*

The advent of mortgage-backed securities in the 1970s and the subsequent financialization of real estate notes transformed them into highly tradable assets. This period also saw the rise of digital technology, which streamlined note trading and management, making it more efficient and accessible.

- *2008 Financial Crisis and Beyond:*

The subprime mortgage crisis highlighted the risks inherent in the securitization of real estate notes, leading to a reevaluation of lending practices and investment strategies. In the aftermath, there has been a renewed focus on the fundamentals of note investing, emphasizing due diligence, risk assessment, and the pursuit of stable returns.

- *2010 Dodd-Frank Wall Street Reform and Consumer Protection Act*

The regulatory landscape underwent significant changes post-2008, most notably with the enactment of the Dodd-Frank Wall Street Reform and Consumer Protection Act in 2010. This sweeping legislation addressed the root causes of the financial crisis and prevented future systemic failures in the banking and mortgage sectors. One of the primary objectives of Dodd-Frank was to enhance consumer protections and promote economic stability through stricter oversight and regulation.

Implementing the Dodd-Frank Act had far-reaching implications for real estate note investors. The creation of the Consumer Financial Protection Bureau (CFPB) under Dodd-Frank introduced a new regulatory authority responsible for enforcing federal consumer financial laws and ensuring fair lending practices. This law meant lenders operating in the private lending market were subject to heightened scrutiny and required to adhere to more stringent standards, particularly underwriting practices and borrower qualifications.

Additionally, Dodd-Frank introduced Qualified Mortgages (Q.M.), which set forth criteria for loans to be considered safe and sound. While this provided clarity and stability to the mortgage market, it also limited the availability of certain loan products, particularly those catering to borrowers with non-traditional income sources or credit profiles.

The regulatory changes by Dodd-Frank necessitated adjustments in note investing strategies and risk management approaches. Investors had to navigate a more complex regulatory environment, which required increased due diligence and compliance efforts and potentially impacted investment returns. However, these regulations also mitigated systemic risks and promoted a more sustainable and transparent real estate lending market in the long run.

Despite the challenges posed by regulatory changes, the fundamental principles of note investing remained intact. Investors continued to prioritize sound underwriting practices, collateral valuation, and risk mitigation strategies to protect their investments and generate consistent returns. Moreover, the lessons learned from the 2008 financial crisis underscored the importance of adaptability and resilience in navigating market fluctuations and regulatory developments.

As we reflect on the evolution of real estate note investing, it is evident that the sector has undergone significant transformation in response to economic, regulatory, and technological shifts. Yet, the core principles of prudent risk management, diligent due diligence, and a focus on value preservation have remained constant throughout history. Investors must remain vigilant and proactive in adapting to changing market dynamics and regulatory requirements while leveraging emerging opportunities to optimize their investment strategies and achieve long-term success.

Understanding Note Investing:

Note investing remains one of the most misunderstood and underutilized strategies. Demystifying note investing, addressing common misconceptions and fears, and providing evidence-based clarity on why it can be a lucrative component of a well-rounded investment portfolio is accomplished through education. Picking up this book is the first step on our note investment journey.

There is a pervasive belief that note investing is excessively risky and complicated. This misconception stems from a need to understand better how note investing works and the different strategies to mitigate risk. The scale of this problem is significant, as it prevents many potential investors from exploring an avenue that could enhance their investment returns. The implications of this issue are far-reaching, potentially leading to missed opportunities for wealth generation and financial security.

If this problem remains unresolved, the adverse outcomes are multifaceted. Investors may continue to invest in lower-yielding investments, missing out on the higher returns that investing can offer.

Additionally, the broader economy needs to catch up on the liquidity and financial stability the note investing market can provide. Data from the mortgage and finance industries show that note investments when managed correctly, have the potential to offer returns that significantly outpace traditional stock and bond investments.

Transitioning to the solution is the key to unlocking the benefits of note investing, which lies in education and strategic risk management. By understanding the types of notes available, such as performing and nonperforming notes, and the legal and financial frameworks surrounding them, investors can make informed decisions that align with their risk tolerance and investment goals.

Implementation of this solution involves several steps. First, investors should seek educational resources from reputable sources to build a solid foundation of knowledge about note investing. Next, developing a network of experienced note investors and professionals can provide guidance and mentorship. Finally, starting with smaller, less risky investments allows investors to gain experience and confidence.

One potential implementation challenge is the initial learning curve, which most individuals can address through patience and continual learning. As investors become more familiar with note investing, they can gradually explore more complex strategies.

While other solutions, such as traditional investments or speculative markets, may seem safer or more exciting, they often offer a different balance of risk and return than educated note investing can provide. Ultimately, investors can unlock a powerful tool for wealth generation by addressing the misconceptions and fears surrounding note investing with informed strategies and risk management.

A Tale of Two Investors:

To illuminate the comparative analysis further, let's delve into a case study that juxtaposes two investors: John, who ventures into real estate notes, and Sarah, who opts for the stock market route. This examination is set against the backdrop of the volatile economic landscape of the early 2020s, characterized by uncertainty and fluctuating market conditions. A seasoned real estate investor, John pivoted towards investing in real estate notes after recognizing the potential for stable, passive income.

With a background in property management, John's transition was backed by a solid understanding of the real estate market's intricacies. Sarah, on the other hand, is a stock market enthusiast. With an MBA and a keen interest in market trends, Sarah has always been attracted to the dynamic nature of stocks, viewing them as a pathway to significant returns.

The primary challenge both investors faced was navigating the uncertainty of the early 2020s economic landscape. John was concerned about the real estate market's stability and borrowers' ability to meet loan obligations. Sarah's challenge was the stock market's volatility, exacerbated by economic fluctuations and global events affecting company valuations.

John's strategy involved meticulous research into the real estate market, focusing on properties in economically stable regions with growth potential. He also diversified his investment across different types of real estate notes to spread the risk. Embracing the stock market's volatility, Sarah diversified her portfolio across various sectors, relying on a mix of long-term investments in blue-chip stocks and short-term trades based on market trends.

The outcomes for both investors were telling. Thanks to his careful selection and diversification, John experienced a steady ROI of 8% annually, with none of his notes defaulting. While seeing highs of up to 20% returns, Sarah's portfolio also faced significant downturns, with an overall annual ROI of 5% after accounting for losses.

This case study reveals the inherent stability of real estate notes compared to the stock market. John's investment yielded consistent returns with lower volatility, a testament to the secured nature of real estate notes. While potentially more lucrative, Sarah's journey carried higher risk and required more active management to navigate the market's ups and downs.

Critics might argue that real estate notes limit the potential for high returns compared to the stock market's limitless possibilities. However, this case study underscores the value of stability and predictability in investment, particularly in uncertain economic times. It highlights the importance of aligning investment choices with risk tolerance and financial goals.

In drawing parallels between John's and Sarah's experiences, we see a clear depiction of real estate notes' comparative stability and profitability. This case study reinforces the earlier foundational knowledge and provides practical insights into the strategic considerations and outcomes of investing in real estate notes versus stocks. It exemplifies the broader narrative of investment strategies, emphasizing the significance of stability and predictability in achieving long-term financial goals.

CHAPTER 3

Identifying Investments and Due Diligence

Why Notes? The Stability Factor:

Real Estate Notes vs. Stocks:

The allure of real estate notes and stocks stands out, each presenting its rewards and challenges. Real estate notes offer an investment secured by the physical asset of property, providing a tangible safeguard. Conversely, stocks represent a share in a company's fortunes, their value swaying with its performance and broader market trends.

This analysis aims to peel back the layers of these investment avenues, evaluating their stability and financial appeal. It highlights the relative strength of real estate notes against the stock market's volatility, guiding investors toward informed decisions that match their risk tolerance and financial goals. We will explore risk exposure, return on investment (ROI), market volatility, and the impact of economic shifts.

Both real estate notes and stocks can offer passive income streams, yet they demand thorough market understanding and research. While they share this requirement for success, their paths diverge significantly regarding income stability, risk profile, and response to market changes. Real estate notes typically feature fixed interest rates, leading to more predictable, stable returns. The inherently less volatile nature of real estate ensures a steady cash flow. In contrast, the stock market is prone to swift changes, making it susceptible to sudden drops in value influenced by market sentiment, company performance, and global economic trends, thus presenting a higher risk.

Economic downturns highlight the resilience of real estate notes, secured by tangible assets, offering a buffer against total loss.

Conversely, stocks can see pronounced losses during economic strife, exemplifying their vulnerability. This comparison showcases the steadier nature of real estate notes. It prompts a reflection on investment priorities, especially during financial uncertainty. It encourages investors to seek out options that provide both security and predictability.

Real Estate Notes vs. Rental Real Estate:

For a more comprehensive picture, it's crucial to contrast these options with owning rental real estate and landlord challenges. While direct real estate investment can offer tangible assets and the potential for income through rent, it also comes with significant challenges. These include property maintenance responsibilities, dealing with tenant issues, and the potential for costly vacancies. Unlike the hands-off nature of real estate notes, being a landlord requires active management. It can introduce a different spectrum of risks and responsibilities.

Banking vs. Property Ownership:

A note investor is akin to being a bank. The property owner, even a landlord, must make their mortgage payment regardless of any other issues with the property. Understanding these dynamics is crucial in developing a broader investment strategy that aligns with individual financial objectives and risk appetites.

Since you are not the property owner, do not limit yourself to one geographic location. I have notes in Georgia, Tennessee, Oklahoma, New Jersey, Pennsylvania, and Ohio. I just had one recently paid off in North Carolina. Some say it is too risky if you have to foreclose and now have a property in another state. As you will see in one of the case studies in the final chapter of this book, you can leverage your network to work through such issues. I took back a house via foreclosure in Tennessee, did a complete renovation to include adding a bedroom, and sold it again with seller financing without ever setting foot in Tennessee. And I made a hefty profit!

The Paper to Profit Transformation:

Our journey into the world of real estate notes now progresses to a crucial phase: understanding how these notes transform from mere paper transactions to valuable assets that can generate consistent returns.

This transformation is not automatic; it requires insight, diligence, and a strategic approach. In the next two chapters, our goal is to equip you with the knowledge and steps necessary to achieve this transformation, thereby enhancing the value of your investment portfolio through real estate notes.

Prerequisites for this journey include the following:

A basic understanding of real estate and financial principles.

- Access to real estate note opportunities.
- The readiness to engage with these instruments' theoretical and practical aspects.
- A network of knowledgeable professionals, such as note brokers, real estate attorneys, investment advisors, and other experienced note investors.

Transformation Steps:

The process begins with a broad overview, summarizing the steps in transforming real estate notes into valuable assets. Each of these steps is critical in its own right and contributes to the overarching goal of generating consistent returns. These steps include the following:

- **In this chapter:**
- Identifying potential note investments
- Conducting due diligence
- **In the following chapter:**
- Purchasing notes
- Managing notes
- Exiting the investment profitably

Identifying Potential Note Investments:

Identifying potential note investments is a crucial first step in real estate note investing. Investors often purchase notes for less than the unpaid balance left on the note. The difference between the amount the investor pays and the unpaid balance is the total yield from the investment. New note investors will often make the mistake of looking for the most significant yield or the biggest difference in the price they will pay for the note and the unpaid balance left on the note. Typically, the bigger the discount on the note, the more issues the note will have. For example, a note with a considerable discount may have paperwork problems that could expose the investor to additional risk. A general rule of thumb to use, particularly if you are a new investor, is that the bigger the discount in the note - the more significant the difference between what you pay for the note and the unpaid balance left on the note - the more substantial the risk involved. Investors who focus only on yield, excluding other aspects of the note, might pass up lucrative investment opportunities.

Let's explore the multifaceted process of scouting the market for viable opportunities and uncovering notes that align with your investment criteria.

Define Your Investment Criteria:

Before entering the market, it is crucial to establish specific investment criteria that align with your risk tolerance, financial objectives, and preferred investment strategy. Take into account the following factors:

- Desired yield or return on investment
- Risk tolerance, ranging from low-risk performing notes to higher-risk nonperforming notes
- Investment timeframe and liquidity preferences
- Geographic preferences or targeted markets

Exploring Available Note Types:

Real estate notes come in various forms, offering unique risk and return profiles. Explore different note types to determine which aligns best with your investment objectives.

- *Performing Notes:*

Performing notes stand out as a beacon of stability and reliability. With their solid payment history and consistent borrower repayments, these notes offer investors a lower-risk option than their nonperforming counterparts. Yet, despite the lower risk profile, performing notes still present an opportunity for moderate returns, making them an attractive choice for investors seeking a balance between risk and reward.

Imagine a scenario where a borrower diligently meets their repayment obligations, adhering to the terms of the loan agreement without fail. Month after month, the investor receives a steady income stream from interest payments, providing a predictable cash flow that can be relied upon to cover expenses, reinvest, or diversify into other opportunities. This stability and predictability are the hallmarks of performing notes, offering investors peace of mind and financial security.

The benefits of investing in performing notes extend beyond stability and predictability. With lower default risk and consistent income generation, investors can enjoy the added advantage of capital preservation and portfolio resilience. By including performing notes in a diversified investment portfolio, investors can mitigate risk, enhance returns, and achieve a more balanced and sustainable investment strategy.

However, investing in performing notes requires careful consideration and due diligence. Investors must conduct thorough research to assess the creditworthiness of borrowers, evaluate the quality of underlying collateral, and understand the terms of the loan agreement. By undertaking comprehensive due diligence, investors can identify high-quality performing notes and minimize risk in their investment portfolio.

Furthermore, investors should explore various exit strategies for performing notes, such as holding the note to maturity, selling it on the secondary market, or refinancing the loan. Evaluating these options allows investors to adapt to changing market conditions and optimize investment returns.

Performing notes offers investors a compelling opportunity to achieve stability, income generation, and lower risk in the dynamic world of real estate investing.

- *Nonperforming Notes:*

Nonperforming notes present a unique set of challenges and opportunities. Unlike their performing counterparts, nonperforming notes involve borrowers who have defaulted on their loan payments, leading to uncertainty and increased risk for investors. However, within this risk lies the potential for substantial returns through successful resolution strategies such as loan modification, short sale, or foreclosure.

Picture a scenario where a borrower has fallen behind on loan payments and cannot meet repayment obligations outlined in the loan agreement. As a result, the note transitions from performing to nonperforming status, signaling a shift in the investment landscape. While this change introduces higher levels of risk, it also opens the door to creative resolution strategies that have the potential to unlock significant value for investors.

One such strategy is loan modification, which renegotiates the loan terms to make repayment more manageable for the borrower. This modification may involve reducing the interest rate, extending the loan term, or forgiving a portion of the principal balance. By working with borrowers to find mutually beneficial solutions, investors can rehabilitate nonperforming notes and restore them to performing status, thereby generating steady income and preserving the value of the investment.

Another resolution strategy is a short sale, where the property securing the note is sold for less than the outstanding balance owed by the borrower. While short sales can result in a loss for investors, they offer an opportunity to liquidate the asset quickly and minimize further losses associated with prolonged non-performance. Additionally, short sales can relieve distressed borrowers and help them avoid foreclosure, which can be a lengthy and costly process for all parties involved.

In cases where resolution through modification or short sale is not feasible, foreclosure may result. Foreclosure involves seizing the collateral property through legal proceedings and selling it to recover the outstanding debt. While foreclosure can be a complex and time-consuming process, it allows investors to force the sale of the property to recover the legal amount of money owed on the loan. This monetary recovery includes all legal costs for the foreclosure. If the property sells at auction, any proceeds realized beyond what is owed to the lender go to other lien holders or the borrower.

Investing in nonperforming notes requires a thorough understanding of the risks and rewards involved and the strategies for resolution and asset management. By implementing effective resolution strategies, investors can mitigate risk, maximize returns, and unlock the hidden value within nonperforming notes.

While nonperforming notes carry higher risk than performing notes, they also present opportunities for substantial returns through strategic resolution strategies.

Utilizing Multiple Sourcing Channels:

To identify potential note investments, leverage a diverse range of sourcing channels:

- *Online Platforms:*

In today's digital age, sourcing real estate notes has become more accessible and convenient than ever, thanks to specialized online platforms dedicated to buying and selling notes. These platforms serve as virtual marketplaces, connecting investors with a broad inventory of real estate notes and providing essential tools for due diligence and transaction facilitation.

Imagine having access to a vast array of real estate notes, all available for exploration and evaluation from the comfort of your home. Specialized online platforms offer investors seeking to diversify their portfolios and capitalize on the opportunities presented by the real estate note market precisely this.

These online platforms act as centralized marketplaces where investors can browse, filter, and analyze real estate notes based on their specific criteria and investment objectives. Whether you're looking for performing or nonperforming notes, residential or commercial properties, first or junior liens, there's a note for every investor preference and risk appetite.

One key advantage of sourcing notes from online platforms is the wealth of information and tools available to investors to conduct due diligence. Detailed listing descriptions, property profiles, borrower information, financial data, and historical performance metrics provide valuable insights into the underlying assets and help investors make informed investment decisions.

Many online platforms offer sophisticated analytical tools and calculators to help investors assess each note's potential returns and risks. From cash flow projections and yield calculations to risk assessment models and scenario analysis, these tools empower investors to evaluate the viability of a note investment and identify opportunities for value creation.

Transaction facilitation is another critical aspect of sourcing notes from online platforms. These platforms streamline the entire investment process, from initial discovery and due diligence to negotiation, documentation, and closing. By providing secure and efficient transactional infrastructure, online platforms facilitate seamless communication and collaboration between buyers and sellers, reducing friction and accelerating deal execution.

Investors must exercise caution and diligence when sourcing notes from online platforms. While these platforms offer convenience and accessibility, they also present risks, such as incomplete or inaccurate information, undisclosed liabilities, or fraudulent listings. To mitigate these risks effectively, investors should conduct thorough due diligence, verify the credibility and reputation of the platform and its users, and seek professional guidance when necessary.

In conclusion, specialized online platforms dedicated to buying and selling real estate notes offer investors unprecedented access to diverse investment opportunities. By leveraging the tools and resources available on these platforms, investors can evaluate potential investments and execute transactions confidently and efficiently. With the right approach and diligence, sourcing notes from online platforms can be valuable for building a successful real estate note investment portfolio.

- *Marketing Campaigns:*

Launching targeted marketing campaigns can be a powerful strategy for connecting with 'mom and pop' note owners looking to liquidate their assets. By leveraging direct mail, email marketing, and networking events, investors can effectively reach potential sellers and uncover hidden opportunities in the market.

Imagine casting a wide net to identify individuals or families who own real estate notes but want to exit their investments for various reasons. These 'mom and pop' note owners may be seeking liquidity, facing financial challenges, or simply looking to simplify their investment portfolio. By positioning yourself as a knowledgeable and trustworthy buyer, you can offer solutions to their needs while capitalizing on valuable investment opportunities.

Direct mail campaigns are a tried-and-true method for reaching potential note sellers. Direct mail pieces can capture recipients' attention and prompt them to consider selling their notes. Personalized letters, postcards, or brochures tailored to the recipient's circumstances and motivations can yield impressive results, driving engagement and generating leads for potential note acquisitions.

Email marketing is another effective strategy for connecting with note owners and initiating conversations about potential transactions. Building a targeted email list of note owners and sending informative and compelling messages can pique their interest and open the door to further discussions. Providing valuable insights, highlighting your expertise, and offering solutions to their needs can help establish rapport and credibility, laying the groundwork for future deals.

Networking events offer invaluable opportunities to connect with note owners face-to-face and build relationships within the industry. Attending real estate conferences, investor meetups, or industry-specific events allows you to interact with potential sellers, learn about their needs and preferences, and explore possible collaboration opportunities. By actively participating in networking events and engaging with fellow professionals, you can expand your network, uncover off-market deals, and stay ahead of the competition.

Launching a successful marketing campaign requires careful planning, execution, and follow-up. Investing in targeted list-building, crafting compelling messaging, and tracking campaign performance is essential to a successful marketing strategy. Additionally, nurturing leads, building trust, and maintaining ongoing communication with potential sellers are critical for converting leads into successful transactions.

It's vital to approach marketing campaigns with empathy, integrity, and professionalism, respecting potential sellers' needs and circumstances at all times. Building trust and rapport with note owners is key to establishing mutually beneficial relationships and fostering long-term success in real estate note investing.

- *Investment Funds:*

Observing private investment funds or institutional investors can reveal unique opportunities to acquire notes that no longer fit their portfolio objectives. By networking within the industry and staying attuned to market trends, investors can gain insights into potential opportunities and forge valuable connections with key market players.

Imagine tapping into a vast reservoir of institutional capital and expertise, where private equity funds and institutional investors actively manage portfolios of real estate notes. With sophisticated investment strategies and rigorous portfolio management practices, these entities constantly evaluate their holdings and adjust their investment strategies to align with changing market dynamics and portfolio objectives.

As an astute investor, staying informed about the activities and intentions of private investment funds and institutional investors in the real estate note market is essential.

Networking within the industry, attending conferences, and participating in industry forums can provide valuable insights into potential opportunities and emerging trends, allowing investors to position themselves strategically and capitalize on market inefficiencies.

One avenue for sourcing notes from private equity funds or institutional investors is establishing relationships with key decision-makers and portfolio managers within these organizations. By cultivating rapport and demonstrating your real estate note investing expertise, you can be a trusted partner and resource for potential note dispositions. Keeping lines of communication open and staying top-of-mind with these entities can lead to valuable opportunities to acquire notes that no longer align with their investment objectives.

Additionally, monitoring industry publications, news sources, and market reports can provide valuable intelligence on potential note dispositions by private equity funds or institutional investors. By staying abreast of market trends, regulatory changes, and macroeconomic factors impacting the real estate note market, investors can anticipate shifts in investment strategies and identify potential opportunities to acquire notes at attractive terms.

Navigating the landscape of private investment funds and institutional investors requires diligence, patience, and strategic positioning. Understanding their investment objectives, risk tolerance, and exit strategies is crucial for aligning potential note acquisitions with their portfolio needs and investment criteria. By tailoring acquisition proposals to address their specific requirements and preferences, investors can increase their chances of securing favorable deals and building long-term relationships with these entities.

Conduct Due Diligence:

Thorough due diligence is critical before committing to any note investment (we explore due diligence in more detail in the coming chapters.) When evaluating a property, investors must remember that they are purchasing the note, not the property. Refrain from dismissing note opportunities because you would not live on the property. Remember, you are the bank! You are not the property owner! The property is collateral, so look for the condition of the collateral along with all the other due diligence criteria. Also, look for "emotional equity," which means looking for things like a well-kept yard, flowers in flower boxes, and the number of years the borrower has lived there - things that show they have an emotional connection to the property. This connection is a big incentive for them to stay current on their loan - your investment.

Evaluate key factors such as:

- Borrower creditworthiness and payment history.
- Property valuation and condition.
- Equity- determine the loan-to-value ratio.
- Terms of the note.
- Pay history.
- Paperwork- determine the quality of the legal documents.

CONCLUSION:

Identifying potential note investments requires a strategic and multifaceted approach, combining market research, due diligence, and networking within the industry. By defining your investment criteria, exploring diverse note types, leveraging multiple sourcing channels, conducting thorough due diligence, and seeking professional guidance, you can uncover opportunities that have the potential to generate attractive returns while managing risk effectively in the dynamic landscape of real estate note investing.

CHAPTER 4

Purchasing, Managing, and Exiting Notes

Purchasing Notes:

With due diligence completed and your investment decision solidified, purchasing the real estate note is the next step. This phase marks the culmination of your efforts in identifying and evaluating potential investments. However, navigating the purchase process requires careful consideration and attention to detail, particularly regarding acquisition methods and safeguards against possible risks. Let's delve into the intricacies of purchasing a real estate note:

Determine the Purchase Method:

The method of purchasing a real estate note can vary depending on the seller and the specific circumstances surrounding the transaction. Common avenues for acquiring notes include:

Direct Purchase from a Bank:

Sometimes, investors may acquire real estate notes directly from banks or financial institutions holding the underlying loans. This route often involves negotiating with bank representatives or asset managers and adhering to their established procedures for note sales.

Broker-Assisted Purchase:

Note brokers facilitate transactions between buyers and sellers in the real estate note market. Engaging a reputable note broker can provide access to a broader inventory of notes and streamline the purchase process through their expertise and industry connections.

Private Transaction:

Alternatively, you can acquire real estate notes through private transactions negotiated directly with individual sellers, such as distressed homeowners, investors, or note holders. These transactions offer flexibility, but structuring the deal may require thorough due diligence to mitigate risks.

Execute Receivable Purchase and Sale Agreement (RPSA):

The Receivable Purchase and Sale Agreement (RPSA) is a cornerstone document governing the purchase and sale of notes between parties. This legally binding agreement outlines the terms, conditions, and obligations of both the buyer and seller, providing clarity and certainty to the transaction.

The RPSA is your guiding document when purchasing a note. This comprehensive agreement delineates the rights and responsibilities of both parties, ensuring a smooth and transparent transaction from start to finish. Before signing on the dotted line, investors must understand the key components of the RPSA and conduct thorough due diligence to mitigate risks and protect their interests.

The RSPA Typically Includes the Following Elements:

- *Identification of Parties:*

The agreement begins by identifying the buyer, seller, and other relevant parties, such as note servicers, trustees, or attorneys. Clear identification ensures all parties know their roles and responsibilities throughout the transaction.

- *Description of the Note:*

The RPSA provides a detailed description of the purchased real estate note, including the principal amount, interest rate, maturity date, payment terms, and any collateral securing the note. This description ensures that both parties understand the underlying asset and its characteristics clearly.

- *Purchase Price and Payment Terms:*

The purchase price and payment terms are among the most critical components of the RPSA. This section specifies the agreed-upon purchase price for the note. It outlines the payment schedule, including down, installment, or balloon payments. Clarity on payment terms is essential for avoiding misunderstandings and disputes later on.

- *Representations and Warranties:*

The RPSA typically represents the terms made by the buyer and seller regarding the note purchase. These may include assurances about the note's validity, the absence of undisclosed liabilities, and the seller's legal authority to sell the note. Thoroughly reviewing and understanding these representations and warranties is crucial for assessing the integrity of the transaction.

- *Conditions Precedent:*

The RPSA may outline certain conditions precedent that must be satisfied before the transaction can proceed. These conditions may include obtaining necessary approvals, conducting due diligence, or securing financing. Identifying and addressing these conditions at the outset ensures a smooth and timely closing.

- *Closing and Delivery:*

Finally, the RPSA specifies the closing date and outlines the procedures for transferring and delivering the note and related documents. These procedures include instructions for executing closing documents, transferring funds, and recording the transaction. Adhering to the closing and delivery provisions ensures that the transaction is completed per the agreement's terms.

Investors should conduct thorough due diligence to assess the quality and integrity of the note before signing the RPSA. Due diligence may include reviewing the note documents, conducting a title search, assessing the borrower's creditworthiness, and evaluating the underlying collateral. Additionally, consulting with legal and financial professionals can provide valuable insights and guidance to ensure the transaction proceeds smoothly and follows applicable laws and regulations.

Arrange financing (if applicable):

Leveraging financing to purchase notes can be a strategic and lucrative approach for investors seeking to maximize returns and optimize capital utilization. This strategy involves borrowing money at a lower interest rate than the rate of return on the note, allowing investors to capture the difference as profit—a practice commonly referred to as arbitrage.

Arbitrage, in the context of note investing, refers to exploiting differences in interest rates between borrowed funds and the rate of return on the acquired note. By borrowing money at a lower cost than the interest earned on the note, investors can generate positive cash flow and enhance their overall return on investment. This arbitrage opportunity allows investors to amplify their returns without requiring additional capital investment, making it an attractive strategy for optimizing capital efficiency.

Investors must exercise caution and diligence when utilizing financing to purchase notes. Before committing to the acquisition, investors must ensure funding is secured on favorable terms. This includes conducting thorough due diligence on potential lenders, evaluating loan terms and conditions, and assessing the feasibility of the arbitrage opportunity.

One critical consideration when using financing to purchase notes is securing funding before committing to the purchase. If financing falls through after committing to the acquisition, investors risk damaging their reputation and credibility with the seller. Failing to fulfill the purchase agreement due to inadequate funding can sour the relationship with the seller and jeopardize future business opportunities.

To mitigate this risk, investors should prioritize securing financing and obtaining pre-approval from lenders before entering into purchase agreements. By proactively addressing financing requirements and ensuring that funding is in place, investors can proceed confidently and avoid potential pitfalls associated with financing contingencies.

Conduct Closing Procedures:

With the purchase agreement finalized and financing arrangements in place, the next step in acquiring a real estate note is to proceed with the closing procedures. This critical phase of the transaction involves transferring ownership of the note from the seller to the buyer, following all necessary legal and financial requirements.

Depending on the complexity of the transaction and the parties involved, closing procedures may vary, but they typically include the following steps:

Reviewing and Signing Legal Documents:

At the closing table, the buyer and seller review and sign various legal documents related to the transfer of ownership of the real estate note. These documents may include the promissory note, assignment of mortgage or Deed of trust, and any other relevant paperwork outlining the terms and conditions of the transaction. It's essential for both parties to carefully review these documents to ensure accuracy and compliance with the terms of the purchase agreement.

Verifying Financial Calculations:

As part of the closing process, verify all financial calculations related to the transaction to ensure accuracy and completeness. Verification includes prorated payments for property taxes, insurance premiums, other expenses, and adjustments for escrow balances and closing costs. This helps prevent discrepancies and ensures that both parties agree regarding the financial aspects of the transaction.

Facilitating Fund Exchange:

Once all legal documents have been reviewed and signed, the exchange of funds completes the transaction. This typically involves the transfer of funds from the buyer to the seller, facilitated through wire transfers or certified checks. The funds exchanged cover the purchase price of the real estate note, as well as any applicable closing costs and fees. Both parties need to ensure that funds are transferred securely and in accordance with the terms of the purchase agreement.

Preparing and Executing the Allonge:

In addition to the standard legal documents, an allonge may be prepared and executed to accompany the promissory note. An allonge is a separate sheet of paper that extends the promissory note, documenting any endorsements or amendments made. The allonge is signed by the seller and attached to the promissory note, providing a clear record of the change in ownership and any modifications to the note terms.

Notifying the Servicing Company:

As part of the closing process, the buyer must notify the servicing company responsible for managing the real estate note of the change in ownership. This involves providing the servicing company with a copy of the mortgage assignment or Deed of trust and any other relevant documentation confirming the transfer of ownership. Proper notification ensures that the servicing company updates its records accordingly and directs future payments and communications to the new owner of the note.

Record Documents:

After acquiring a real estate note investment, it's imperative to complete the process by recording relevant documents with the appropriate authorities, such as the county recorder's office. This step ensures the legal validity and enforceability of your interest in the underlying property and provides essential protections for your investment. Let's explore the significance of recording documents and the steps involved in this crucial process:

Ensuring Legal Validity:

Recording documents, such as deeds of trust, mortgages, or assignments, with the county recorder's office, is fundamental in establishing legal ownership and interest in real estate properties. By recording these documents, you establish a public record of your rights and interests in the property, protecting your investment from competing claims or disputes.

Establishing Priority:

Recording documents also serve to establish priority among competing interests in the property. In the event of default or foreclosure, recorded documents determine the order in which creditors receive payments from the property sale proceeds. Promptly recording your interest ensures that you maintain a favorable position in the priority chain, enhancing the security of your investment.

The Process of Recording Documents:

Recording documents provides constructive notice to interested parties, including potential buyers, lenders, or other stakeholders, regarding your interest in the property. This public record serves as a deterrent against fraudulent or unauthorized transactions involving the property, preserving the integrity of your investment.

Recording liens with the recorder of records in the jurisdiction where the property is located is a crucial step in securing and protecting the creditor's interest in real estate transactions. This process establishes a public record of the lien, provides notice to third parties of the creditor's claim against the property, and establishes the lien's priority in the hierarchy of liens.

To record liens, investors typically submit the necessary documents, such as a mortgage, Deed of trust, or mechanics lien, to the records office in the county where the property is situated. These documents are reviewed, stamped with a recording date and number, and entered into the public record. It's essential to pay the recording fee at submission and ensure the documents meet the formatting and content requirements specified by state and local laws. Once recorded, the lien becomes a matter of public record. It is accessible to anyone conducting a title search or property inquiry.

Recording documents remotely may pose logistical challenges for investors who reside outside the property's area. However, many recorder of records offices offer online or mail-in recording services to accommodate out-of-area filers.

Investors can typically mail their documents and the required recording fee to the recorder of records office for processing and recording. Some offices also provide electronic recording (e-recording) services, allowing documents to be submitted and recorded electronically through a secure online platform.

In addition to recording liens directly with the records office, investors may also utilize third-party online services for document recording. These services offer convenient and efficient solutions for remote recording, allowing investors to submit documents electronically and track the recording process in real-time. Before using a third-party online service, investors should ensure that it is reputable, secure, and compliant with state and local recording requirements.

Recording liens with the recorder of records is critical to securing creditor's interests in real estate transactions and establishing priority in the hierarchy of liens.

Safeguard Against Fraud:

Real estate note transactions involve significant financial stakes, making it imperative to take precautions to protect against fraudulent activities and scams. With the rise of digital transactions and online platforms, investors must be vigilant and implement robust safeguards to safeguard their investments and personal information.

One of the actions that is susceptible to fraud is the process of wire transfers. Scammers may attempt to intercept wire transfers or deceive investors into wiring funds to fraudulent accounts. To mitigate this risk, investors should implement secure wire transfer protocols, such as using encrypted communication channels, verifying the authenticity of recipient accounts, and confirming the legitimacy of wire transfer instructions through multiple channels. It's also advisable to avoid sharing sensitive financial information over unsecured networks or email, as these channels are vulnerable to hacking and interception.

Another potential area of concern is the online recording of documents, such as mortgage assignments or deeds of trust. Scammers may attempt to forge or alter these documents to fraudulently transfer ownership of real estate notes. To prevent this, investors should utilize reputable and secure online platforms that offer robust authentication and verification measures to record documents. Additionally, investors should carefully review recorded documents for accuracy and completeness and consult with legal professionals to confirm the validity and enforceability of the recorded instruments.

Verifying the legitimacy of the seller of a note is another crucial step in avoiding fraud and scams. Scammers may impersonate legitimate sellers or use fake identities to deceive investors into purchasing fraudulent notes. To verify the authenticity of sellers, investors should conduct thorough due diligence, including verifying the seller's identity, conducting background checks, and confirming ownership of the note through title searches and public records. Additionally, investors should be wary of sellers who pressure them to rush into transactions, refuse to provide documentation, or fail to disclose relevant information about the note.

Furthermore, new investors should consider purchasing notes only from reputable sources, such as established private equity funds or professional note investors with a proven track record. Investing through established funds or seasoned professionals can provide an added layer of security and confidence, as these entities are vested in maintaining their reputation and credibility in the industry. Additionally, it may be safer for new investors to purchase notes through established professionals utilizing hypothecation, as discussed later in this book. Hypothecation allows investors to lend funds to experienced experts who manage the note portfolio on their behalf, providing an added level of oversight and risk management. A note, or note portfolio, is used as collateral for the loan.

Consulting with legal and financial professionals is essential for mitigating the risk of fraud and scams in real estate note transactions. Legal professionals can provide guidance on legal requirements, review documentation, and ensure compliance with regulatory standards. Financial professionals can offer insights into financial risks, assess the legitimacy of counterparties, and provide recommendations for secure transaction protocols. By leveraging the expertise of these professionals, investors can minimize the risk of falling victim to fraud and scams and protect their investments and financial interests.

The purchase process for acquiring a real estate note is a pivotal stage in real estate note investing. By understanding the various acquisition methods, executing a thorough purchase agreement, arranging financing when necessary, diligently conducting closing procedures, and safeguarding against potential risks, investors can confidently navigate the complexities of note acquisitions and ensure the successful completion of transactions.

Managing Notes:

Board the Loan with a Loan Servicing Company:

Boarding a loan with a loan servicing company requires careful coordination and communication. By following the appropriate steps and working closely with the servicing company, you can ensure efficient management and administration of your loan investment. Keep the same servicing in place unless there is a problem with the servicer. Experience shows that changing servicing companies can cause interruptions in payment because the borrower needs clarification about where to send new payments or needs to change their automated payment set-up with their bank.

Ensuring Efficient Management:

Whether you're acquiring a loan that isn't being serviced or transitioning ownership of a loan already under servicing, boarding the loan with a reputable loan servicing company is crucial for efficient management and administration. Let's explore the steps involved in both scenarios:

Loan Not Currently Serviced:

Suppose you've acquired a loan that isn't currently being serviced. In that case, the process of boarding the loan with a loan servicing company involves the following steps:

- *Selecting a Servicing Company:*

Research and identify reputable loan servicing companies that specialize in managing the type of loan you've acquired. Consider experience, reputation, technology capabilities, and pricing structure.

- *Negotiating Servicing Agreement:*

Contact the selected loan servicing company to negotiate the terms of the servicing agreement. These terms include defining responsibilities, service fees, reporting requirements, and any special instructions specific to the loan.

- *Transfer of Loan Data:*

Provide the loan servicing company with comprehensive loan data, including borrower information, payment history, loan terms, and any relevant documentation. Ensure the data's accuracy and completeness to facilitate seamless boarding.

- *Onboarding Process:*

Work closely with the loan servicing company to facilitate onboarding. This may involve training sessions, testing systems and processes, and finalizing service agreements and documentation.

- *Initiating Servicing:*

Once the loan servicing company has completed the onboarding process and verified the loan data, they will begin servicing the loan according to the agreed-upon terms. Monitor the transition closely to ensure a smooth and successful transfer.

Change of Ownership for Serviced Loan:

If you've acquired a loan that a loan servicing company is already servicing, notifying the servicing company about the change of ownership is essential to ensure continuity and compliance. Here's how to proceed:

- *Notification to Servicing Company:*

Notify the current loan servicing company about the change of ownership as soon as possible. Provide them with detailed information about the new owner, including contact information and any updated instructions or preferences.

- *Transfer of Ownership Documentation:*

Prepare and provide the necessary documentation to the loan servicing company to facilitate the transfer of ownership. This may include assignment documents, purchase agreements, and legal notices confirming the change in ownership.

- *Verification and Acknowledgment:*

The loan servicing company will verify the documentation provided and acknowledge the change of ownership. They may require additional information or documentation to complete the transfer process.

- *Transition Period:*

Work closely with the loan servicing company to ensure a smooth transition period. Coordinate necessary actions, such as updating borrower communications, payment instructions, or account access.

- *Review Servicing Agreement:*

Review the existing servicing agreement to ensure that it reflects the updated ownership information and any changes in responsibilities or terms resulting from the transfer.

Why Use a Loan Servicing Company?

Effective management of your note investment is key to realizing its value. Managing involves working with borrowers to ensure timely payments, restructuring the note if necessary, and staying abreast of any changes that could affect the investment's security or return. A professional, licensed servicing company should be servicing your notes. There are many pitfalls when trying to service your own notes that could cost you time, money, and legal fees. Trying to save a few dollars by servicing your own notes can cost you considerably in the long run.

Loan servicing companies are vital in managing and administrating real estate loans, providing essential services to investors and borrowers. Maintaining effective communication with the servicing company is crucial for ensuring transparency, compliance, and efficient resolution of any issues that may arise during the life of the loan. Let's delve into the functions of loan servicing companies and the importance of investor-servicer communication:

Functions of Loan Servicing Companies:

- *Payment Processing:*

One of the primary functions of loan servicing companies is to process borrower payments, including principal, interest, taxes, and insurance. They ensure that payments are accurately recorded, allocated, and disbursed according to the loan agreement terms.

- *Account Administration:*

Loan servicing companies handle all aspects of account administration, including maintaining borrower records, escrow management, and tracking loan balances, payment histories, and other relevant account details.

- *Customer Service:*

Servicing companies serve as borrowers' primary point of contact, providing assistance, answering inquiries, and addressing concerns related to loan servicing, payment options, account information, and other related matters.

- *Escrow Management:*

For loans with escrow accounts, servicing companies manage the collection and disbursement of funds for property taxes, insurance premiums, and other escrowed items. They ensure that payments are made timely and accurately to avoid disruptions or penalties.

- *Default Management:*

In the event of borrower default or delinquency, loan servicing companies oversee loss mitigation efforts, including loan modifications, repayment plans, foreclosure proceedings, and property disposition. They work to protect the interests of both investors and borrowers while adhering to applicable laws and regulations.

- *Compliance and Legal Requirements:*

Maintaining communication with the servicing company is essential for compliance with legal requirements and regulations governing loan servicing. Investors must adhere to laws such as the Fair Debt Collection Practices Act (FDCPA) and the Real Estate Settlement Procedures Act (RESPA), which mandate specific procedures and disclosures in loan servicing.

- *Transparency and Oversight:*

Effective communication with the servicing company allows investors to maintain transparency and oversight over their loan investments. By staying informed about loan performance, borrower interactions, and any issues or concerns, investors can make informed decisions and take proactive measures to protect their interests.

- *Resolution of Issues:*

In case of any discrepancies, errors, or disputes related to loan servicing, maintaining open communication with the servicing company facilitates prompt resolution of issues. Investors can raise concerns, request clarifications, or initiate corrective actions to ensure the integrity and accuracy of loan servicing operations.

- *Online Portals and Communication Channels:*

Many loan servicing companies offer online portals or platforms that provide investors with convenient access to loan information, account details, and communication tools. These portals allow investors to monitor loan activity, view payment histories, access borrower communications, and track real-time account performance.

- *Legal Requirements for Communication:*

Investors are typically prohibited from directly communicating with borrowers regarding loan servicing matters as a matter of law. All communication must go through the servicing company to ensure compliance with legal requirements and protect borrower privacy rights. This restriction helps maintain professionalism, consistency, and compliance with regulatory standards in borrower interactions.

Exploring Exit Strategies for Performing Loans: Maximizing Returns and Flexibility

For note investors, implementing the right exit strategy for performing loans requires careful assessment of investment goals, risk tolerance, and market conditions. Whether selling a partial interest, opting for a total loan sale, or exploring alternative exit options, investors must prioritize maximizing returns, managing risk, and maintaining portfolio flexibility to achieve long-term success in note investing.

While holding onto a performing loan can provide steady cash flow and reliable returns, there are strategic reasons why an investor may choose to exit the investment. Let's explore some common exit strategies explicitly tailored for note investors:

Partial Note Sale:

- *Capital Deployment:*

Selling a partial interest in a performing loan can free up capital for reinvestment in other note opportunities. By liquidating a portion of the investment, investors can seize attractive deals or diversify their portfolio without entirely exiting the existing investment.

Risk Management:

Diversifying investment holdings through the sale of a partial interest helps mitigate concentration risk and safeguard against potential losses. By spreading capital across multiple notes, investors can enhance portfolio resilience and reduce their exposure to individual loan performance.

Full Loan Sale:

- *Profit Realization:*

Selling the entire performing loan allows investors to realize profits and capitalize on accrued interest payments and potential appreciation in the loan's value. By locking in gains, investors can secure returns and reinvest the proceeds into new opportunities or strategic initiatives.

- *Portfolio Optimization:*

Exiting a performing loan through a complete sale enables investors to streamline their portfolio and reallocate resources to higher-yielding investments or assets with better risk-adjusted returns. This strategy helps optimize portfolio performance and aligns with long-term investment objectives.

Alternative Exit Strategies:

- *Note Exchange Programs:*

Some investment platforms offer note exchange programs where investors can trade their existing performing loans for different assets or opportunities. This allows investors to adjust their portfolio holdings and pursue alternative investment strategies without cashing out entirely.

- *Refinancing Considerations:*

While refinancing may not always be the most advantageous strategy for note investors, there may be scenarios in which refinancing the loan benefits both the borrower and investor. For example, suppose the borrower needs a loan modification to avoid default. In that case, the investor may opt for this option over foreclosure.

Partnering with an Expert:

Many investors aspire to take a more passive approach while capitalizing on the opportunities note investing presents. If you are in this category, please seek a trustworthy and experienced note investor with whom to partner. Learning from and leveraging the expertise of an experienced investor can prove invaluable in the long run. You can purchase a partial note from them, offering a level of security as they will support your investment by retaining ownership of the back end of the note. Alternatively, you could enter into a hypothecation agreement, wherein the experienced note investor pledges a note or group of notes as collateral for funds you loan them with an agreed-upon rate of return.

In this hypothecation scenario, a passive investor can receive a specified interest rate monthly, quarterly, or annually. This arrangement is also applicable within an IRA. You can reinvest your interest payment or accept it as cash income, depending on your agreement. It's important to consult with your tax professional regarding structuring such arrangements and ensure that the expert you partner with provides you with a 1099-INT for tax reporting purposes.

As we transition into tips and warnings, we must emphasize the value of patience and due diligence throughout this process. Rushing into investments without proper research can lead to pitfalls such as overpaying for a note or investing in a note with undisclosed problems.

Additionally, staying informed about market conditions and legal considerations can help avoid common mistakes and ensure a smoother investment journey. Consistent returns and the growth of your investment portfolio mark success in transforming real estate notes into valuable assets. Regularly reviewing your portfolio's performance, staying informed on market trends, and being adaptable to changing circumstances are key indicators that you've effectively applied the concepts and strategies discussed.

If you encounter challenges, such as difficulty finding suitable notes or issues with borrowers, consider leveraging professional networks or seeking advice from experienced investors. Solutions often arise from shared knowledge and collaborative problem-solving, ensuring your real estate note investing journey remains profitable and rewarding. You can also be a more passive investor by partnering with an active note investor who will use his or her knowledge and experience to deploy your funds in the best possible manner. You can loan an experienced investor money secured by a note or purchase a partial note. We will explore partial notes later in this book.

Foundational Concepts: Interest Income Explained

Understanding the specific terms and concepts related to interest payments on real estate notes is not just about expanding your financial vocabulary; it's about unlocking the potential to generate significant income through investment. These terms are the foundation upon which real estate investment and note profitability mechanisms are built. By delving into these foundational concepts, we prepare to navigate the complexities of real estate investing with greater confidence and insight.

In this brief section, we'll explore key terms such as 'Interest Rate,' 'Principal,' 'Amortization,' and 'Yield to Maturity,' each of which plays a crucial role in determining the profitability of real estate notes as investment vehicles. This exploration will clarify these terms and demonstrate how they interconnect to affect investors' overall return on investment (ROI).

- *Interest Rate*

Our journey into the intricacies of real estate note investment begins with defining the 'Interest Rate.' In its most basic form, the interest rate is the cost of borrowing money, expressed as a percentage of the principal. It's akin to renting money, where the interest rate dictates the rent price. This rate is pivotal in calculating the income generated from real estate notes, as it directly influences the amount of money an investor receives beyond the repayment of the principal amount loaned.

- *Principal*

Next, we delve into the concept of 'Principal.' The principal represents the amount of money lent on which the interest is calculated. Understanding the principal is crucial because it's the baseline upon which the profitability of the loan is assessed. It's the core amount around which all transactions and interest calculations revolve, akin to the foundation of a building.

- *Amortization*

Following the principle, 'Amortization' is a term that requires our attention. It refers to spreading out a loan's repayment over time in fixed installments. This concept is essential for investors to grasp because it dictates the schedule by which the principal and interest are paid back, influencing the cash flow and the timing of income from the investment. Amortization is like a roadmap for the repayment of the loan, detailing every turn and straightaway until the full repayment destination is reached.

- *Yield to Maturity*

Lastly, 'Yield to Maturity'(YTM) is a critical term that encapsulates the total return anticipated on a real estate note if it is held until its maturity date, considering all interest payments and the repayment of the principal. YTM offers a comprehensive view of the investment's profitability, incorporating the interest income and any gains or losses incurred if the note was purchased at a discount or premium to its face value. It's the ultimate measure of a real estate note's investment performance, akin to calculating the total distance traveled on a journey, considering all the ups and downs.

CONCLUSION:

As a note investor, you must remember that each payment combines the principal amount returned and the interest payment. New note investors often make the mistake of looking at the entire payment received as their cash flow or profit. I use three different approaches as borrowers make payments on notes I own. For some notes, I will look at the amortization schedule and separate the principal and interest amounts. I will then reinvest the principal amount as soon as practical. I will treat the interest payment as my cash flow or profit.

For other notes, I will set aside the entire payment, calculating how long it will take me to recoup the principal amount invested. I will reinvest this as soon as practical to keep my principal working. Once I have recovered my principal, I can see the remainder note as my cash-flowing profit. Finally, I will collect payments and reinvest the entire amount as soon as practical to compound my interest. It is critically important to estimate how much annual tax you will pay on the interest income so you can set this aside for your tax payment at the end of the year.

As we reflect on these terms, consider how they apply to your investment strategies or experiences. How might the interest rate affect your decisions on which real estate notes to invest in? In what ways does understanding amortization change your perspective on the cash flow from these investments? And how does knowing the yield to maturity influence your long-term investment goals? These reflections are not merely academic exercises but practical considerations that can significantly impact your investment outcomes.

By connecting these defined terms to the larger narrative of real estate note investing, we lay the groundwork for a deeper exploration of this lucrative field. These concepts are not isolated islands of knowledge but interconnected parts of a cohesive whole, each contributing to formulating a robust investment strategy.

As we move forward, keep these definitions in mind, for they will serve as critical reference points, guiding our exploration of how to effectively generate income through real estate notes, navigate risks, and ultimately achieve our financial goals. This foundation is not just the first step in our journey; it's the compass that will guide us through the complexities and challenges of real estate note investing, leading us toward informed and profitable investment decisions.

CHAPTER 5

Blueprints for Success: Strategy and Planning

Crafting Your Investment Plan:

Define Your Investment Objectives:

Start by clearly defining your investment objectives. Ask yourself why you are investing in notes. Are you looking to generate passive income to supplement your monthly cash flow? Are you aiming to build long-term wealth through capital appreciation? Or are you seeking to diversify your investment portfolio to reduce overall risk? Understanding your overarching investment objectives will help shape your note-investing strategy and guide your decision-making process.

Establish Clear, Measurable Goals:

Once you've identified your investment objectives, establish clear and measurable goals to achieve them. Specify what you want to accomplish with your note investments. Do you have a target annual income you wish to achieve from your note portfolio? Are you aiming for a certain level of capital growth over a specific time horizon? By quantifying your goals, you can track your progress and hold yourself accountable to your investment plan.

Consider Cash Flow Needs:

In addition to long-term wealth accumulation, consider incorporating cash flow objectives into your note investing goals. Determine how much passive income you need to supplement your monthly expenses or achieve specific financial milestones. Assess your current financial situation, including your existing sources of income and expenses, to determine the role of cash flow in your note investment strategy. Setting realistic cash flow targets will help ensure that your note investments contribute to your overall financial well-being.

Determine Desired Rate of Return and Risk Tolerance:

Evaluate your desired rate of return and risk tolerance to align your note investing goals with your financial capabilities and risk preferences. Determine the level of return you aim to achieve from your note investments, considering factors such as prevailing market conditions, interest rates, and economic outlook. Assess your comfort level with risk and volatility, recognizing that higher returns often come with increased risk. Understanding your risk tolerance and return expectations allows you to tailor your note investment strategy to suit your circumstances.

Set Investment Time Horizon:

Consider your investment time horizon when setting goals for your note investments. Determine whether you have short-term or long-term investment objectives. Short-term goals involve generating immediate cash flow or capitalizing on short-term market opportunities, while long-term goals may focus on wealth accumulation and retirement planning. Establishing a clear investment time horizon will help you choose appropriate investments and implement a suitable investment strategy.

Creating a Strategy:

Crafting a sound strategy is essential for success in note investing. Your level of involvement—whether you're an active or passive investor—will significantly influence your strategy and approach. Here's how to create a plan tailored to your preferred level of involvement:

Assessing Your Level of Involvement:

Before investing in notes, it's crucial to assess your level of involvement in the investment process and determine whether you prefer an active or passive approach.

- *Active Investor:*

If you're an active investor, you're willing to devote time, effort, study, and expertise to manage your note investments actively. This may involve sourcing and acquiring notes, performing due diligence, managing loan servicing, and implementing workout strategies for nonperforming loans. As an active investor, you'll need a deep understanding of note investing principles, market dynamics, and legal considerations.

Your strategy will focus on hands-on management and optimization of your note portfolio to achieve your investment objectives.

- *Passive Investor:*

If you're a passive investor, you prefer a more hands-off approach to note investing. You're looking to deploy your investment capital without actively managing day-to-day operations. Instead, you rely on experienced professionals—such as note investors or servicers—to handle the complexities of note investing on your behalf.

Your strategy may involve purchasing partial notes, where you partner with an expert investor to acquire a fractional interest in a note, or engaging in hypothecation, where you lend funds to experienced investors in exchange for secured interest payments. As a passive investor, you focus on generating passive income and achieving your financial goals with minimal time and effort.

Diversification: A Safety Net

Portfolio diversification in note investing is a vital strategy for those involved in the financial markets, particularly within the note investing niche. Let's break down this concept for clarity.

Portfolio diversification is investing in various assets to reduce exposure to risk associated with any single investment. This principle is akin to the adage 'Don't put all your eggs in one basket,' offering a straightforward definition emphasizing mitigating risk through variety.

In the realm of note investing, diversification involves spreading investments across different types of notes, such as performing notes (those paying on time), nonperforming notes (those in default), and other asset classes (residential, commercial, etc.). It also extends to diversification within note grades, geographic locations of the underlying assets, and issuers. This strategy is crucial because it addresses the inherent unpredictability of markets and borrower behavior. Historically, diversification traces back to the early practices of merchants and investors who spread their resources across various ventures to protect against loss in any endeavor.

This principle has evolved over centuries and has become a cornerstone of modern investment philosophy. Portfolio diversification in note investing fits into a more significant financial management strategy to optimize returns while minimizing risks. It is particularly significant in this niche due to the direct correlation between the performance of the underlying assets (the properties or projects) and the return on the notes. By diversifying, investors can safeguard against localized economic downturns, industry-specific downturns, or defaults on individual loans.

In practice, diversification in note investing might involve holding a mix of residential mortgage notes, commercial real estate notes, and land notes. This mix not only spreads risk but also allows for the potential capture of gains across different market cycles and economic conditions.

However, a common misunderstanding is the assumption that diversification guarantees protection against loss. It's important to clarify that diversification can significantly reduce risk but cannot eliminate it. The key is to manage and understand the levels of risk involved with different types of investments and adjust one's portfolio accordingly.

Leveraging IRA Funds for Note Investing:

In the complex investing world, the quest for stable returns softens individuals' exploration of various avenues. Real estate notes present a unique opportunity, especially when funded through a Roth IRA. This approach combines the tax advantages of Roth IRAs with the potential for steady, passive income from real estate notes, but it comes with its own challenges and nuances.

The primary issue is the underutilization of Roth IRAs for investments beyond the traditional stock market. Many investors need to know that their Roth IRA can be a vehicle for investing in real estate notes, a form of lending where the investor acts as the bank, financing others' real estate purchases. The scale of this underutilization is significant, as it affects the diversity and potential resilience of investment portfolios.

The implications are far-reaching, impacting investors' ability to weather market volatility and achieve long-term financial goals. If left unresolved, this lack of diversification can lead to suboptimal investment outcomes. Portfolios heavily weighted in stocks or mutual funds may experience greater volatility and risk.

These portfolios can suffer during downturns, affecting investors' retirement savings and financial security. On the other hand, real estate notes can provide a steady stream of income regardless of stock market fluctuations, offering a cushion during economic instability. Your IRA account can act like a bank, lending money to qualified borrowers who repay the loan over time with a set interest rate.

The solution to risk mitigation lies in educating investors on the benefits and process of using funds from a Roth IRA to invest in real estate. This approach diversifies investment portfolios and takes advantage of the tax-free growth and withdrawals from Roth IRAs. The reasoning is solid: by combining the stable, passive income potential of real estate notes with the tax benefit of Roth IRAs, investors can enhance their portfolio's performance while managing risk.

Be sure to place your IRA with a company that specializes in self-directed accounts and has an account manager familiar with note investing. Implementation involves a few key steps. First, investors must ensure their Roth IRA is self-directed, which allows investment in a broader range of assets, including real estate notes. Next, identifying reputable platforms or partners for purchasing real estate notes is crucial, as is conducting due diligence on each investment. Potential challenges include navigating the rules regarding self-directed IRA investments and finding quality notes to invest in. These can be addressed through education, professional advice, partnering with a seasoned investor, and careful investment selection. Past outcomes from investors who have taken this route are promising. Case studies show that investing Roth IRA funds in real estate notes has diversified portfolios and provided a steady, tax-advantaged income stream.

These successes underscore the viability of this strategy for achieving long-term financial goals. While other solutions, such as direct real estate or REIT investments, offer similar benefits, they do not always provide the same control or tax advantages as investing in real estate notes through a Roth IRA. Direct real estate investment requires significant capital and management, and REITs, while more passive, do not offer the tax benefit of Roth IRA investments. This makes real estate notes a compelling option for those looking to maximize their investment returns while minimizing taxes.

Calling in Your Team of Experts:

Building Your Note Investing Team:

Investing in real estate notes is a collaborative endeavor. It requires collaboration with a diverse team of professionals who bring unique expertise to the table. By assembling a team of experts, you gain access to valuable insights, resources, and support that can enhance your investment strategy and mitigate risks.

Legal Counsel:

Legal counsel is pivotal in establishing and maintaining asset protection structures such as limited liability companies (LLCs), trusts, or other entities. These structures help shield investors' personal assets from potential liabilities associated with their real estate investments. An attorney specializing in asset protection can advise on the most suitable structure based on individual needs and circumstances.

You may have multiple firms to serve your needs: one for asset protection and legal structures and another specializing in real estate matters. You also may need a referral to an attorney in the state where your note investment is located.

Selecting Legal Counsel for Note Investing:

- *Expertise in Real Estate and Note Matters:*

Real estate note investing involves complex legal considerations, including loan documentation, title issues, and foreclosure procedures. An attorney with expertise in real estate and note matters can provide valuable guidance throughout the investment process and ensure compliance with relevant laws and regulations.

- *State-Specific Legal Representation:*

Legal requirements vary by state, and investors may need to retain legal counsel in the state where the real estate is located. Having legal representation familiar with state-specific laws and procedures is essential for protecting investors' interests in the event of borrower default or foreclosure proceedings.

- *Loan Servicer Referrals:*

Loan servicers, who administer mortgage loans on behalf of investors, can often refer investors to legal counsel when needed. Loan servicers typically have established relationships with legal professionals specializing in real estate and note investing, making it easier for investors to access their required expertise.

CPA (Certified Public Accountant):

Selecting the right CPA is a critical decision for real estate note investors. You can benefit from strategic advice and guidance beyond tax preparation by choosing a CPA with expertise in note investing, a client portfolio including note investors, and a proactive approach to financial planning. Your CPA should serve as a trusted advisor who helps you navigate the complexities of note investing and achieve your financial goals with confidence.

Let's delve into the details of choosing a CPA who not only understands note investing but also provides strategic advice beyond tax preparation:

Selecting a CPA for Note Investing:

- *Industry Knowledge:*

Look for a CPA with in-depth knowledge and experience in real estate note investing. They should be knowledgeable about the unique tax implications, accounting principles, and financial strategies relevant to note investments.

- *Specialization in Note Investing:*

Seek out a CPA specializing in serving note investors with a track record of working with clients in the real estate note investment space. A CPA with expertise in note investing understands the industry's intricacies and can provide tailored advice to meet your needs.

- *Strategic Advisor:*

Choose a CPA who acts as a strategic advisor, not just a financial historian who completes tax returns. Your CPA should offer proactive guidance on tax planning, structuring investments, maximizing deductions, and optimizing your overall financial strategy to align with your investment goals.

- *Client Portfolio:*

Inquire about the CPA's client portfolio to ensure they have note investors as current clients. Working with a CPA serving other note investors indicates their familiarity with the industry and ability to address the unique challenges and opportunities that note investing presents.

- *Future Planning:*

Your CPA should be proactive in helping you develop and execute plans for your note investment portfolio. This includes tax-efficient exit strategies, estate planning considerations, wealth preservation tactics, and succession planning to ensure your long-term financial success.

- *Continuing Education:*

Choose a CPA who actively engages in continuing education and stays updated on changes in tax laws, accounting standards, and industry trends relevant to note investing. A commitment to ongoing learning demonstrates their dedication to providing their clients with the highest level of service.

- *Communication Style:*

Consider the CPA's communication style and accessibility. You should feel comfortable discussing your financial goals, concerns, and questions with your CPA, and they should be responsive and attentive to your needs.

Benefits of a CPA with Note Investing Expertise:

- *Tax Optimization:*

A CPA with note investing expertise can help you navigate complex tax laws and identify opportunities to minimize tax liabilities while maximizing deductions and credits.

- *Financial Planning:*

They can assist in developing a comprehensive financial plan that aligns with your investment objectives, risk tolerance, and timeline. This may include retirement planning, cash flow management, and investment diversification strategies.

- *Risk Management:*

A knowledgeable CPA can help you assess and mitigate risks associated with note investing, such as regulatory compliance, financial reporting accuracy, and asset protection strategies.

- *Strategic Decision-Making:*

Your CPA can empower you to make informed decisions that optimize investment returns and drive long-term financial success by providing valuable insights and analysis.

Bookkeeper:

Selecting the right bookkeeper is essential for maintaining accurate financial records and optimizing the efficiency of your real estate note investing operations. By choosing a bookkeeper who understands the nuances of note investing, communicates effectively with your CPA, and demonstrates proficiency in bookkeeping tasks, you can ensure the integrity of your financial records and lay a solid foundation for financial success.

Let's explore the process of selecting a bookkeeper for real estate note investing, emphasizing the importance of effective communication with your CPA and the distinction between the roles of bookkeeper and CPA:

Selecting a Bookkeeper for Real Estate Note Investing:

- *Understanding the Role of a Bookkeeper:*

A bookkeeper is responsible for maintaining accurate financial records, recording transactions, reconciling accounts, and organizing financial data. Their primary focus is on day-to-day bookkeeping tasks to ensure the accuracy and integrity of your financial records.

- *Cost-Effectiveness Compared to CPA:*

While a CPA offers specialized tax planning and financial strategy expertise, they may not be the most cost-effective option for routine bookkeeping tasks. Hiring a dedicated bookkeeper can be more economical, allowing you to allocate resources efficiently while ensuring accurate financial record-keeping.

- *Effective Communication with CPA:*

Select a bookkeeper who understands the importance of effective communication with your CPA. Clear and timely communication ensures accurate financial reporting, tax compliance, and strategic financial planning.

- *Introduction to CPA (if not already working together):*

If your bookkeeper and CPA do not already work together, facilitate an introduction. Establishing a collaborative relationship between the two professionals ensures seamless coordination and alignment of financial processes, goals, and strategies.

- *Bookkeeper's Expertise in Note Investing:*

Choose a bookkeeper familiar with the unique aspects of real estate note investing. While less specialized than a CPA, a bookkeeper with experience in note investing can better understand the nature of your transactions, categorize income and expenses accurately, and maintain relevant financial records.

- *Attention to Detail and Accuracy:*

Look for a bookkeeper who demonstrates attention to detail and a commitment to accuracy in their work. Real estate note investing involves complex financial transactions, and precise record-keeping is essential for tracking performance, analyzing returns, and preparing reports for stakeholders.

- *Technology Proficiency:*

Consider the bookkeeper's proficiency with accounting software and technology platforms in real estate note investing. A bookkeeper comfortable with industry-standard software can streamline processes, improve efficiency, and enhance the quality of financial reporting.

Benefits of Hiring a Dedicated Bookkeeper:

- *Cost Savings:*

A bookkeeper is often more cost-effective than using a CPA for routine bookkeeping tasks, allowing you to optimize your expenses and allocate resources strategically.

- *Specialized Expertise:*

A bookkeeper with experience in note investing can provide valuable insights and support tailored to the unique requirements of your investment portfolio, enhancing the quality and accuracy of your financial records.

- *Efficient Operations:*

By delegating bookkeeping responsibilities to a dedicated professional, you can streamline financial processes, improve efficiency, and free up time to focus on core investment activities and strategic decision-making.

- *Collaboration with CPA:*

A dedicated bookkeeper works closely with your CPA to ensure accurate financial reporting, tax compliance, and strategic financial planning. Effective communication between the two professionals facilitates seamless coordination and alignment of financial goals and strategies.

Real Estate Note Sourcing Specialist:

Including a real estate note-sourcing specialist on your team can significantly enhance your ability to identify, evaluate, and acquire real estate notes from reputable sources. Their specialized knowledge, deal-sourcing capabilities, and industry connections can provide a competitive advantage in real estate note investing, enabling you to build a robust and profitable note portfolio.

Selecting a Real Estate Note Sourcing Specialist:

- *Access to Note Inventory:*

A real estate note sourcing specialist, often affiliated with a private equity fund or bank has access to a wide range of real estate notes that are available for purchase. They specialize in sourcing distressed debt, performing loans, and other real estate notes from various sources, including financial institutions, distressed asset sellers, and loan originators.

- *Due Diligence Expertise:*

They possess expertise in conducting due diligence on potential note acquisitions and assessing factors such as loan performance, collateral quality, borrower creditworthiness, and legal compliance. Their thorough analysis helps identify high-quality investment opportunities and mitigate risks.

- *Negotiation Skills:*

A skilled note-sourcing specialist can negotiate favorable terms and pricing on behalf of investors when acquiring real estate notes. They leverage their industry knowledge, relationships, and deal structuring capabilities to secure attractive investment opportunities.

- *Deal Structuring:*

They assist investors in structuring note acquisitions to optimize returns and minimize risks. Strategies like loan modifications, workout agreements, or portfolio diversification may enhance the note portfolio's performance.

- *Market Insights:*

They provide valuable insights into market trends, asset pricing dynamics, and real estate note investment strategies. Their market intelligence helps investors make informed decisions and adapt their investment strategies to changing market conditions.

- *Networking Opportunities:*

Real estate note-sourcing specialists often have extensive networks within the industry, including relationships with banks, servicers, brokers, and other professionals. They can facilitate introductions and connections with key stakeholders, expanding investors' access to opportunities and resources.

Loan Servicing Company:

Loan servicing companies are vital in managing and administrating real estate loans, providing essential services to investors and borrowers. Maintaining effective communication with the servicing company is crucial for ensuring transparency, compliance, and efficient resolution of any issues that may arise during the life of the loan. Let's delve into the functions of loan servicing companies and the importance of investor-servicer communication:

Functions of Loan Servicing Companies:

- *Payment Processing:*

One of the primary functions of loan servicing companies is processing borrower payments, including principal, interest, taxes, and insurance. They ensure that payments are accurately recorded, allocated, and disbursed according to the loan agreement terms.

- *Account Administration:*

Loan servicing companies handle all aspects of account administration, including maintaining borrower records, managing escrows, tracking loan balances, tracking payment histories, and other relevant account details.

- *Customer Service:*

Servicing companies serve as borrowers' primary point of contact, providing assistance, answering inquiries, and addressing concerns related to loan servicing, payment options, account information, and other matters.

- *Escrow Management:*

For loans with escrow accounts, servicing companies manage the collection and disbursement of funds for property taxes, insurance premiums, and other escrowed items. They ensure these payments are made timely and accurately to avoid disruptions or penalties.

- *Default Management:*

In the event of borrower default or delinquency, loan servicing companies oversee loss mitigation efforts, including loan modifications, repayment plans, foreclosure proceedings, and property disposition. They work to protect the interests of both investors and borrowers while adhering to applicable laws and regulations.

Importance of Communication with a Loan Servicing Company:

- *Compliance and Legal Requirements:*

Maintaining communication with the servicing company is essential for complying with legal requirements and regulations governing loan servicing. Investors must adhere to laws such as the Fair Debt Collection Practices Act (FDCPA) and the Real Estate Settlement

Procedures Act (RESPA), which mandate specific procedures and disclosures in loan servicing.

- *Transparency and Oversight:*

Effective communication with the servicing company allows investors to maintain transparency and oversight over their loan investments. By staying informed about loan performance, borrower interactions, and any issues or concerns, investors can make informed decisions and take proactive measures to protect their interests.

- *Resolution of Issues:*

In case of any discrepancies, errors, or disputes related to loan servicing, maintaining open communication with the servicing company facilitates prompt resolution of issues. Investors can raise concerns, request clarifications, or initiate corrective actions to ensure the integrity and accuracy of loan servicing operations.

- *Online Portals and Communication Channels:*

Many loan servicing companies offer online portals or platforms that provide investors with convenient access to loan information, account details, and communication tools. These portals allow investors to monitor loan activity, view payment histories, access borrower communications, and track real-time account performance.

- *Legal Requirements for Communication:*

As a matter of law, investors are typically prohibited from directly communicating with borrowers regarding loan servicing matters. All communication must go through the servicing company to ensure compliance with legal requirements and protect borrower privacy rights. This restriction helps maintain professionalism, consistency, and compliance with regulatory standards in borrower interactions.

Mentors:

Mentorship provides invaluable guidance and support from experienced professionals who have navigated the complexities of real estate note investing. A mentor can offer insights, share best practices, and help you avoid common pitfalls, accelerating your learning curve and increasing your chances of success.

Importance of Mentorship in Real Estate Note Investing:

- *Accountability and Motivation:*

A mentor holds you accountable for your actions, goals, and progress, motivating you to stay focused, disciplined, and committed to your investment strategy. Their encouragement and feedback help you overcome challenges, maintain momentum, and achieve your objectives.

- *Network and Connections:*

Mentorship provides access to a broader network of industry professionals, investors, and experts, facilitating connections and collaboration opportunities. Networking with like-minded individuals can lead to partnerships, joint ventures, and exclusive real estate note investment opportunities.

- *Risk Mitigation:*

Learning from a mentor's experiences and expertise helps mitigate real estate note investing risks. By leveraging their knowledge and insights, you can make more informed decisions, identify potential risks, and implement risk mitigation strategies to protect your investments.

- *Continuous Learning and Growth:*

Mentorship fosters a culture of continuous learning and personal growth, encouraging you to expand your knowledge, skills, and capabilities as a real estate note investor. By embracing new ideas, perspectives, and strategies, you can adapt to changing market conditions and position yourself for long-term success.

Beware of Online Gurus and Social Media Advice:

Quality of Information:

Exercise caution when seeking advice from online gurus or individuals on social media platforms. Not all sources of information are reliable or trustworthy, and misinformation or misleading advice can lead to costly mistakes in your investment journey.

Lack of Accountability:

Online gurus may lack accountability for their advice, and their recommendations may not be based on real-world experience or proven expertise in real estate note investing. Verify the credentials and track record of individuals offering advice online before relying on their guidance.

Overhyped Promises:

Be wary of overhyped promises or get-rich-quick schemes touted by online gurus. Real estate note investing (and any other type of investing) requires patience, diligence, and strategic planning. Success is often the result of careful analysis, prudent decision-making, and disciplined execution over time.

Choosing a Reputable Mentor or Organization:

- *Reputation and Track Record:*

Look for mentors or organizations with a proven reputation and track record of success in real estate note investing. Research their credentials, testimonials, case studies, and client reviews to assess their credibility and reliability.

- *Industry Experience:*

Choose mentors or organizations with extensive experience and real estate note investing expertise. Consider factors such as their knowledge of the market, investment strategies, and track record of successful transactions in the note space.

- *Education and Training Programs:*

Evaluate the quality of education and training programs the mentor or organization offers. Look for comprehensive curricula, interactive learning opportunities, and ongoing support to help you develop the knowledge and skills necessary for success in real estate note investing.

- *Community and Resources:*

Assess the mentor or organization's commitment to building a supportive community of investors and providing access to valuable resources, tools, and networks. A strong community can enhance your learning experience, foster collaboration, and provide opportunities for growth and development.

A Recommended Mentor Organization:

- *NoteSchool and Eddie Speed:*

NoteSchool, led by Eddie Speed, is a reputable organization known for its expertise in real estate note investing. With over 40 years of experience in the industry, *NoteSchool* offers comprehensive education and training programs, mentorship opportunities, and access to a supportive community of investors. Eddie Speed's track record of success and commitment to empowering investors make *NoteSchool* a trusted resource for individuals looking to excel in real estate note investing.

I have been a member of *NoteSchool* for many years, and I have made hundreds of thousands of dollars from this ongoing investment in education. Your education continues beyond one class or seminar. The investing landscape changes, sometimes rapidly, so ongoing investment for even experienced investors is critical.

CONCLUSION:

Building Your Dream Team:

Assembling your team of experts is a strategic investment in your success as a real estate note investor. Each team member brings specialized knowledge and skills, complementing your strengths and empowering you to achieve your investment goals. Whether you are a seasoned investor or just starting out, surrounding yourself with knowledgeable professionals is the key to unlocking your full potential in real estate note investing.

CHAPTER 6

Diving Into Notes: The Legalities

Navigating the Legal Landscape:

This section of the book gives a broad overview of some of the legal issues involved in note investing. It is not meant to be all-inclusive or to replace competent legal advice.

The legal landscape of real estate investing is as varied as it is complex. From the Dodd-Frank Wall Street Reform and Consumer Protection Act to the Fair Debt Collection Practices Act, each piece of legislation introduces myriad regulations that dictate how investments can be structured, serviced, and, ultimately, how profitable they can be. The intricacies of these laws can seem daunting, but they hold the key to unlocking successful investment strategies.

If you have a general understanding of the laws and regulations affecting your investments, you will recognize when there is an issue that you need to explore further during due diligence, and you will recognize which documents you will need your attorney to review. You will also understand the importance of having your documents drafted or reviewed by an attorney who is conversant in real estate and note investing in particular.

Take, for instance, the Dodd-Frank Act, which has reshaped the landscape of consumer lending and investing. Its provisions impact real estate notes' origination, servicing, and purchase, especially in owner-financed transactions. For investors, navigating this regulatory maze requires more than just an understanding of the law but an ability to anticipate how changes in these regulations can impact their investment portfolio.

Dodd-Frank Act:

Before delving into the intricacies of note investing, it's crucial to understand how legislation like the Dodd-Frank Wall Street Reform and Consumer Protection Act plays a pivotal role. Enacted in July 2010, the Dodd-Frank Act is a comprehensive piece of financial reform legislation aimed at reducing risk within the financial system, primarily through increased regulation of financial institutions and the creation of new agencies tasked with overseeing various components of the financial market.

The Dodd-Frank Act was introduced in response to the 2007-2008 financial crisis to prevent a similar catastrophe. It focuses on enhancing consumer protection, increasing transparency, and promoting stability within the financial system. The Act's broad scope encompasses rules affecting banks, mortgage lenders, and, significantly, investors dealing in notes and other debt instruments.

One of the critical components of the Dodd-Frank Act relevant to note investing is its regulation of mortgage lending and the requirement for lenders to assess a borrower's ability to repay before issuing a loan. Additionally, it has provisions that affect the trading of securities and derivatives, including notes.

Historically, regulating financial instruments and the entities that trade them has evolved from a lightly regulated marketplace to one under significant scrutiny and control. This evolution mirrors the increasing complexity of financial markets and their products. The Dodd-Frank Act is part of this historical trend, aiming to fill regulatory gaps made evident by the economic crisis.

The Dodd-Frank Act mandates adherence to specific consumer protection standards and reporting requirements in note investing. This means that investors must be mindful of how these regulations impact the purchasing, servicing, and selling of notes, ensuring compliance to avoid legal and financial penalties.

Real-world applications of these regulations include note investors needing to work closely with licensed servicing companies that comply with the Dodd-Frank Act to manage their notes, especially if they involve residential mortgages. This compliance ensures that the servicing of the note aligns with federal standards for consumer protection, which can include everything from how payment collections are handled to how modifications to the terms of a note are executed. You should use a licensed servicing company with a good track record. The modest fees you pay for this service are well worth the peace of mind of knowing that you comply with all applicable laws and regulations.

A common misunderstanding related to the Dodd-Frank Act is that it applies only to banks or large financial institutions. However, its reach extends to individual investors and smaller entities involved in financial transactions, including those dealing in notes. These investors must understand that non-compliance can result in significant penalties, underscoring the importance of familiarizing oneself with the Act's requirements and integrating them into investment strategies.

State-specific regulations further complicate this landscape. What's permissible in one state may be restricted in another, affecting everything from the interest rates you can charge to the methods you can pursue delinquent borrowers. The diversity of these regulations means that a one-size-fits-all approach to note investing is not just ineffective; it's potentially hazardous. Investors must tailor their strategies to align with each state's legal constraints and opportunities.

Moreover, compliance is not a static requirement but a dynamic challenge that evolves with legislative changes, court rulings, and shifts in regulatory priorities. Keeping abreast of these changes is crucial. Failure to comply can result in significant legal liabilities, financial penalties, and even the forfeiture of rights over the invested asset. Yet, within these challenges lie opportunities; for those well-versed in legal and regulatory nuances, navigating these complexities can provide a competitive edge.

For example, understanding the specifics of foreclosure laws can expedite the recovery process for non-performing notes, minimizing losses and maximizing returns. Similarly, familiarity with the legalities of loan modifications and debt restructuring can enable investors to rehabilitate non-performing loans, transforming potential losses into profitable assets.

The role of legal counsel in this process cannot be understated. Partnering with attorneys specializing in real estate and finance law is a safeguard and a strategic investment. These professionals can guide compliance, offer strategies for risk mitigation, draft documents, and represent investors in legal proceedings, ensuring that their interests are protected in the face of regulatory challenges.

In essence, the legal and regulatory landscape of real estate note investing is a critical component that shapes the strategies and success of investors. By mastering this aspect, investors protect their current investments and position themselves to capitalize on opportunities others may overlook due to the complexities involved. This mastery requires diligence, adaptability, and a proactive approach to legal education and compliance—a trifecta distinguishing successful investors in the competitive arena of real estate notes.

Usury Laws:

Usury laws vary by jurisdiction, with each state or country setting its limits on allowable interest rates. These laws define usurious interest rates and establish the legal consequences for violating these limits.

Usury laws set the maximum interest rates lenders can charge on loans. These rates may be expressed as a percentage of the principal loan amount or as an annual percentage rate (APR). Lenders must be aware of the applicable usury limits in their jurisdictions. Violating usury laws can have serious legal consequences for lenders.

Some potential penalties include:

- *Voiding of the Note:*

If a lender charges interest rates that exceed the legal limit set by usury laws, the entire loan agreement may be deemed void or unenforceable. This means that the lender may lose the right to collect any interest or principal on the loan.

- *Refund of Interest Paid:*

In cases where usury laws are violated, borrowers may be entitled to a refund of any interest payments they've made in excess of the legal limit. This can result in financial losses for the lender and erode the profitability of the loan. For an investor purchasing notes, checking the usury laws before investing may reveal that the interest rate on the note in question is in violation. An unsuspecting investor purchasing such a note could find themselves refunding years of interest to a borrower - interest the previous owner of the note collected.

- *Civil Liability:*

Lenders who violate usury laws may face civil lawsuits from borrowers seeking damages for usurious interest charges. These lawsuits can result in monetary judgments against the lender, including the repayment of unlawfully charged interest and possibly additional penalties.

- *Criminal Charges:*

In some jurisdictions, egregious violations of usury laws may constitute criminal offenses. Lenders guilty of criminal usury may face fines, imprisonment, or other criminal penalties.

- *Exceptions and Exemptions:*

Usury laws often include exceptions or exemptions for certain loans or lenders. For example, federal preemption laws may exempt loans from federally regulated banks or credit unions from state usury limits. Additionally, some states have specific exemptions for certain types of loans, such as mortgages or small business loans.

Compliance Measures:

To avoid running afoul of usury laws, lenders should take proactive measures to ensure compliance, including:

- *Legal Review:*

Before extending a loan, lenders should seek legal advice to ensure the loan terms comply with applicable usury laws.

- *Interest Rate Caps:*

Lenders should carefully structure loan agreements to ensure that the interest rates charged are within the legal limits set by usury laws.

- *Documentation:*

Proper documentation of loan terms, including interest rates and repayment schedules, can help demonstrate compliance with usury laws in a legal dispute.

- *Monitoring Regulatory Changes:*

Usury laws may change, so lenders should stay informed about updates or amendments to ensure ongoing compliance.

The Truth in Lending Act (TILA):

Enacted in 1968 and subsequently amended, TILA ensures that consumers receive clear and accurate information about the terms and costs associated with credit transactions. The law applies to most types of consumer credit, including credit cards, mortgages, and personal loans.

Compliance with TILA's Disclosure requirements is essential for lenders to avoid civil liability, regulatory enforcement actions, and the potential right of rescission for borrowers. By understanding and adhering to TILA's provisions, lenders can promote transparency and fairness in consumer credit transactions.

- *Disclosure Requirements under TILA:*

TILA mandates that lenders provide borrowers with certain critical disclosures before the consummation of a credit transaction. These disclosures include:

- *Annual Percentage Rate (APR):*

Lenders must disclose the APR, which represents the actual cost of borrowing expressed as an annual percentage rate. The APR includes the interest rate and specific fees and charges associated with the loan.

- *Finance Charges:*

Lenders must disclose the total finance charges associated with the loan. Changes may include any interest, fees, and other charges that the borrower must pay over the life of the loan.

- *Total Amount Financed:*

Lenders must disclose the total amount financed, which represents the principal loan amount minus any prepaid finance charges.

- *Total of Payments:*

Lenders must disclose the total amount the borrower will have paid by the end of the loan term, including principal, interest, and any other finance charges.

- *Payment Schedule:*

Lenders must provide a payment schedule showing the number, frequency, and amount of payments the borrower must make over the loan's life.

- *Right of Rescission:*

One of the critical provisions of TILA is the right of rescission for certain types of transactions. Under TILA, borrowers can rescind certain credit transactions within a specified period, typically three business days after the transaction consummation or receipt of the required disclosures, whichever occurs later. This right allows borrowers to cancel the transaction and receive a full refund of any fees or charges paid.

Penalties for Non-Compliance:

Failure to comply with TILA's disclosure requirements can seriously affect lenders. Some potential penalties include:

- *Civil Liability:*

Lenders who fail to provide the required disclosures may be liable for civil penalties, including statutory damages and attorneys' fees. Borrowers may also have the right to bring a private lawsuit against the lender for violations of TILA.

- *Right of Rescission:*

Suppose a lender fails to provide the required disclosures or violates TILA's provisions. In that case, the borrower may have the right to rescind the transaction, even after the loan is funded.

- *Regulatory Enforcement:*

Regulatory agencies, such as the Consumer Financial Protection Bureau (CFPB), can enforce TILA and penalize lenders that have violated it.

Compliance Measures:

To ensure compliance with TILA, lenders should take proactive measures, including:

- *Disclosure Review:*

Lenders should carefully review and ensure borrowers receive all required disclosures per TILA's requirements.

- *Training:*

Training staff members involved in the loan origination process on TILA's requirements can help prevent compliance errors.

- *Record-keeping:*

Maintaining accurate records of loan transactions and disclosure documents can help demonstrate compliance during an audit or regulatory investigation.

- *Monitoring Regulatory Updates:*

Staying informed about changes or updates to TILA and related regulations can help lenders adapt their practices to remain compliant.

State Specific Regulations:

State-specific regulations play a significant role in governing lending practices, and understanding these regulations is crucial for lenders to ensure compliance. It is essential to review the laws in the state where a note you are originating or purchasing resides.

Here are two examples of state-specific laws that impact lending practices:

Example 1: Usury Laws in California

Like many other states, California has usury laws that limit the maximum interest rates lenders can charge on loans. However, California's usury laws are particularly noteworthy for their complexity and the potential consequences of non-compliance.

- *California Constitution Article XV Section 1:*

This provision sets the maximum allowable interest rate for most consumer loans at 10% annually. However, numerous exceptions and exemptions exist, such as loans made by banks, credit unions, and licensed finance lenders, subject to different interest rate limits.

- *California Finance Lenders Law (CFL):*

The CFL regulates the activities of finance lenders and brokers operating in California. Lenders licensed under the CFL are subject to specific requirements regarding interest rates, fees, disclosures, and other aspects of lending practices.

- *California Deferred Deposit Transaction Law (CDDTL):*

Also known as the payday lending law, the CDDTL imposes restrictions on payday loans, including limits on loan amounts, fees, and rollovers. Lenders must comply with the requirements of the CDDTL when offering payday loans to California consumers.

Example 2: Mortgage Licensing Laws in New York

New York has stringent regulations governing mortgage lending activities, including licensing requirements for mortgage brokers, lenders, and servicers. These regulations protect consumers and ensure the integrity of the mortgage lending market.

- *New York Banking Law Article 12-E:*

This statute, also known as the Mortgage Brokerage Registration Act, requires individuals and entities engaged in mortgage brokerage activities to register with the New York Department of Financial Services (DFS).

Registered mortgage brokers must meet specific competency and ethical standards and adhere to strict disclosure requirements.

- *New York Real Property Law Article 12-A:*

This law governs mortgage loan originators (MLOs) and sets forth licensing, education, testing, and ongoing continuing education requirements for MLOs operating in New York. MLOs must be licensed by the DFS and comply with all applicable laws and regulations.

- *New York General Obligations Law Section 5-501:*

This provision restricts certain types of high-cost home loans, including limits on interest rates, fees, and prepayment penalties. Lenders must ensure compliance with Section 5-501 when originating high-cost home loans in New York.

CHAPTER 7

Diving Into Notes: Acquisition

Where to Find Real Estate Notes:

R eal estate notes present an intriguing opportunity to build a diversified and robust investment portfolio. These financial instruments, representing secured loans on real estate properties, offer a unique mix of security and profitability.

Understanding where to find these notes is crucial for investors aiming to tap into this market. This section will explore the platforms and networks where real estate notes are available for sale, providing a roadmap for investors to navigate this landscape.

- *Online Market Places:*

Online Marketplaces have become a primary channel for investors purchasing real estate notes. These platforms offer a wide range of listings from various sellers, including banks, private lenders, and other investors. They provide detailed information about each note, such as the interest rate, term, and security backing the loan, enabling investors to make informed decisions. These marketplaces also offer tools and resources to help investors analyze potential investments. It is critical to remember that many private investors will sell notes in these Marketplaces the same way people sell used cars.

Just as you may not know if a used car has significant problems without being inspected by a qualified mechanic, you may only know a note has issues if you have the documents reviewed by an expert. You know how to examine all aspects during your due diligence phase. This is another reason to partner with a seasoned investor; they may have access to sources of notes that general investors do not. Many seasoned note investing experts will have a relationship with a group or private equity fund that has quality notes to select from based on your parameters.

Going it alone may be like buying a used car from a private seller or a used car lot. Note that sellers rarely offer warranties. It is buyer beware.

- *Peer-to-Peer Lending Platforms:*

Peer-to-peer (P2P) Lending Platforms have gained popularity as a source of real estate notes. These platforms connect individual borrowers with investors, bypassing traditional banking systems. Investors can fund a portion of the loan or the entire amount, depending on their investment strategy and capital availability. P2P platforms offer a range of real estate-backed loans, from residential to commercial, providing a diverse selection for investors. Detailed due diligence is crucial when buying P2P loans.

- *Banks and Financial Institutions:*

Banks and Financial Institutions often sell non-performing or distressed notes to recover outstanding debts. These sales can be direct purchases from the bank or through auctions. Investing in these types of notes can be riskier but also offer the potential for higher returns. Again, investors need to conduct thorough due diligence when considering these investments.

- *Note Brokerages:*

Note Brokerages specializes in the sale and purchase of real estate notes. Working with a brokerage can simplify finding and acquiring notes, as they typically have a vast network and a deep understanding of the market. Brokerages can also provide valuable services such as due diligence, note valuation, and negotiation assistance. Be sure to research the brokerage thoroughly. Many will sell their best quality notes to seasoned buyers with an ongoing relationship, leaving slim pickings for the one-off investor.

- *"Mom and Pop" Notes:*

"Mom and Pop" notes are also a possibility as a source of notes. Sometimes, you will run across someone who owns a note that they don't know what to do with. They may have acquired it when they seller-financed their own home, or they may have inherited it. These can be good opportunities. You may have to educate the seller and negotiate a price for the note, as the holder may not know anything about note investing. They may want to sell it at full price - the unpaid balance amount (UPB.) You should explain in detail why the note is not worth the full UPB because of the quality of the paperwork, the collateral, or the payment history. It also may be worth buying a partial note (more on this later.)

The Art of the Deal: Purchase Price Criteria

Pricing a real estate note involves comprehensively evaluating various criteria impacting its value and marketability. From the condition of the collateral property to the note's legal status and supporting documents, several factors must be considered to determine an appropriate price for a note.

- *Condition of Collateral Property:*

The condition of the collateral property, also known as the underlying asset, plays a significant role in determining the value of a real estate note. Properties in good condition with high market value are more desirable collateral and may command higher prices for the associated note. Conversely, properties in poor condition or with significant defects may lower the note's value and increase investors' perceived risk.

- *Legal Status of Note and Supporting Documents:*

The legal status of the note and supporting documents, such as the mortgage or deed of trust, can impact its price and marketability. Notes with unambiguous terms, properly executed documents, and valid liens on the collateral property are more attractive to investors and may command higher prices. Conversely, notes with legal issues, such as missing or defective documents, disputed ownership, or unresolved title issues, may be discounted due to increased risk and uncertainty.

- *Interest Rate and Payment History:*

The note's interest rate and payment history are key factors in determining its value. Notes with higher interest rates and a consistent payment history are more desirable to investors and may command higher prices. Conversely, notes with below-market interest rates or a history of missed or late payments may be discounted to reflect the increased risk of default.

- *Remaining Term of the Note:*

The note's remaining term, or the time until it reaches maturity, can impact its price. Notes with longer remaining terms may attract investors seeking stable, long-term cash flow and command higher prices. Conversely, notes with shorter remaining terms may be discounted to reflect the reduced duration of future payments and the potential for reinvestment risk.

- *Market Conditions and Interest Rates:*

Market conditions and prevailing interest rates can influence the pricing of real estate notes. In a low-interest-rate environment, investors may be willing to pay higher prices for notes to achieve higher yields relative to other investment opportunities. Conversely, in a high-interest-rate environment, investors may demand higher returns and be more selective in their note purchases, leading to lower prices for notes.

- *Borrower Creditworthiness and Financial Stability:*

The creditworthiness and financial stability of the borrower are important considerations for investors evaluating real estate notes. Borrowers with solid credit profiles and stable financials are more likely to make timely payments and fulfill their obligations under the note, reducing the risk of default and increasing the perceived value of the note.

- *Market Demand and Investor Preferences:*

Market demand and investor preferences also determine the pricing of real estate notes. Notes in high-demand markets or with desirable features, such as low loan-to-value ratios or seasoned payment histories, may command higher prices due to increased competition among investors. Conversely, notes with less desirable attributes or in niche markets may be discounted to attract buyers.

Negotiating the Price:

When investors are sourcing real estate notes, it's important to remember that each source will have unique pricing policies. Whether acquiring notes from a private equity fund, an online note listing service, or other sources, understanding these policies and navigating the negotiation process is essential for securing favorable deals.

- *Private Equity Funds:*

Private equity funds typically have established pricing policies based on their internal valuation models and investment criteria. In many cases, there may be little room for negotiation on price, as the fund manager sets a fair value for the notes based on their risk assessment, return potential, and market conditions. Investors sourcing notes from private equity funds can expect transparency and consistency in pricing, with little opportunity for haggling over price.

- *Online Note Listing Services:*

Online note listing services, where various note sellers post notes for sale, often involve more flexibility in pricing and more significant opportunities for negotiation. Sellers may set asking prices based on their assessment of the note's value, market conditions, and desired return on investment. When negotiating with sellers on these platforms, investors must tactfully point out various reasons for discounting the asking price, such as the collateral property's condition, the borrower's creditworthiness, or other factors affecting the note's value.

- *Direct Sellers and Note Brokers:*

When sourcing notes directly from individual sellers or note brokers, pricing negotiations can vary widely depending on the seller's motivations, financial situation, and market knowledge. Some sellers may be open to negotiation and willing to adjust their asking.

Price is based on the investor's assessment of the note's value and perceived risks. Others may have fixed pricing policies or be less willing to negotiate, particularly if they are confident in the quality and marketability of the note.

- *Distressed Note Sales:*

Pricing negotiations may be more complex in distressed note sales, where notes are sold at a discount due to default, foreclosure, or other financial challenges. Investors may need thorough due diligence to assess the underlying risks and determine an appropriate purchase price. Negotiating with distressed note sellers requires sensitivity, empathy, and a keen understanding of the seller's motivations and constraints.

- *Secondary Market Platforms:*

Secondary market platforms, where institutional investors and noteholders trade existing notes, may have their own pricing dynamics and negotiation processes. Investors sourcing notes through these platforms may encounter varying levels of transparency and liquidity, as well as different pricing models and negotiation strategies.

CONCLUSION:

Navigating the world of real estate notes requires a blend of strategy, knowledge, and due diligence. Whether sourcing notes from online marketplaces, peer-to-peer platforms, banks, brokerages, or individual sellers, each avenue presents unique opportunities and challenges.

Understanding the nuances of negotiation in this market is crucial. Investors must determine the motivation of the note seller, which will then determine the approach when negotiating a price. Doing solid research and investigation is critical since many sellers will not be forthcoming about any negative issues affecting the quality of the note. Just as you would not purchase a house without a thorough property inspection, you would not want to purchase a note without a detailed inspection of all its components. Doing so will position you to capitalize on this market's diverse and lucrative opportunities.

CHAPTER 8

Due Diligence: Acquisition Criteria

The Borrower:

U nderstanding the borrower is paramount in real estate note investing, particularly within legal constraints surrounding accessing credit history. Here's a comprehensive guide on what to investigate and alternative methods for obtaining pertinent borrower information:

- *Income Verification:*

Request documentation from the note seller or loan servicer to verify the borrower's income and employment stability. This may include pay stubs, tax returns, or employment verification to ensure the borrower can meet payment obligations.

- *Asset Verification:*

Review the documentation the note seller or loan servicer provides regarding the borrower's asset position. This may include information on real estate properties the borrower owns, savings, investments, or retirement accounts.

- *Liabilities and Debt-to-Income Ratio:*

While direct access to the borrower's credit report is restricted, evaluate the borrower's debt-to-income ratio through the documentation provided by the note seller or loan servicer. Analyze the borrower's monthly debt obligations compared to their documented gross monthly income.

- *Legal and Regulatory Checks:*

Conduct thorough checks using publicly available records for any legal or regulatory issues involving the borrower. Search for lawsuits, judgments, or liens that may impact the borrower's financial stability and ability to fulfill obligations under the note.

- *Investigative Methods:*

Given the limitations on accessing the borrower's credit history, real estate note investors must utilize alternative methods for due diligence:

- *Seller Disclosure:*

Request disclosure documents from the note seller, including any information they have about the borrower's credit history, financial status, and payment behavior.

- *Third-Party Services:*

Engage third-party services specializing in borrower due diligence, such as background checks and asset verification services. While credit reports may not be accessible, these services can provide valuable insights into the borrower's background and financial standing.

- *Professional Networks:*

Utilize professional networks, such as real estate agents, attorneys, and property managers, who may know or have insight into the borrower's background and financial standing.

The Collateral:

In real estate note investing, the property serving as collateral is pivotal for securing investments. It is essential to understand its physical condition and market value, even within legal constraints. Many new to note investing will pass on a note because they would never "live in that house." Keep in mind that you are the bank, not the owner! If everything else in the other categories of due diligence looks good, don't dismiss the note for this reason. Here's how note investors can gather crucial information about the collateral:

- *Broker's Price Opinion (BPO):*

Given restrictions on property inspections, a Broker's Price Opinion (BPO) offers a suitable alternative. This involves a licensed real estate broker or agent assessing the property's exterior condition and market value. While not as comprehensive as a full inspection, a BPO provides valuable insights into the property's condition and potential value. Engage a qualified real estate broker or agent specializing in the property's area to provide a BPO. They'll evaluate the property's exterior condition, review comparable sales data, and consider market trends to determine its value.

This valuation serves as a vital reference point for assessing the property's worth in the event of default. Often, a BPO can be found in the note's collateral file. Check the date to be sure it is current, but do not place undue weight on a BPO. Often, they are not accurate. If you need more precise information, consider calling a local real estate agent, explain what you are doing, and ask if they can provide any guidance on prices in the neighborhood. They will often be happy to help.

Methods to Gather Information:

- *Online Resources:*

Utilize real estate websites (Zillow, Redfin, Realtor.com, and the like), public records databases, and property valuation tools to supplement BPO findings. While not a substitute for professional assessment, these resources offer additional data and context for evaluating the property's value.

Equity:

In real estate note investing, assessing the equity in the property is crucial for understanding the borrower's incentive to maintain payments and mitigate the risk of default. During the 2008 real estate lending crisis, many borrowers walked away from properties when their equity was insufficient to cover their mortgage obligations. Here's how note investors can determine the equity in the property:

- *Loan-to-Value (LTV) Ratio:*

Calculate the loan-to-value ratio by dividing the outstanding loan balance by the property's current market value. A lower LTV indicates higher quality in the property. For example, if the property's market value is $200,000 and the outstanding loan balance is

$150,000, the LTV ratio is 75%, leaving 25% equity in the property.

- *Home Equity Lines of Credit (HELOCs) and Second Mortgages:*

Consider any existing HELOCs or second mortgages on the property. These additional liens reduce the available equity for the primary lender. Assess the total debt secured by the property to determine the net equity available to cover the primary note.

- *Foreclosure Proceeds:*

Evaluate potential foreclosure proceeds in the event of default. If the property were foreclosed, the net proceeds after satisfying liens and expenses would determine the available equity. Understanding this potential outcome is critical for assessing risk and recovery options.

Terms:

Understanding the terms of the note is crucial in real estate note investing, as they dictate the repayment schedule, interest rates, and potential risks associated with the investment. Here's a comprehensive exploration of the various aspects to consider:

- *Amortization Schedule:*

Review the note's amortization schedule to understand how principal and interest payments are structured over the loan term. Assessing the amortization schedule helps determine the borrower's repayment ability and the timing of cash flows for the investor.

- *Interest Rate:*

Examine the interest rate specified in the note to understand the borrower's cost of borrowing and the investor's potential return. Consider whether the interest rate is fixed or variable and evaluate its competitiveness compared to prevailing market rates regarding the borrower's ability to obtain a conventional bank loan.

- *Loan Term:*

Evaluate the loan term's duration to assess the investment's length and the timing of cash flows. Longer loan terms may provide more consistent cash flows but expose the investor to interest rates and market risks over an extended period. Verify how many months are remaining on a note being purchased.

- *Balloon Payments:*

Check for any provisions for balloon payments within the note. Balloon payments require the borrower to pay off the remaining loan balance in a lump sum at a specified date, potentially leading to refinancing or selling the property to cover the payment.

- *Prepayment Penalties:*

Determine whether the note includes prepayment penalties. Prepayment penalties impose fees on borrowers for paying off the loan before the scheduled maturity date. They can affect the borrower's flexibility and the investor's expected returns.

- *Escrow Accounts:*

Review whether the note requires the borrower to contribute to escrow accounts for property taxes, insurance, or other expenses. Escrow accounts help ensure these obligations are paid on time, reducing the risk of default due to unpaid taxes or insurance premiums.

- *Default Provisions:*

Understand the default provisions outlined in the note, including conditions triggering default, grace periods, and remedies available to the investor in case of default. Explicit default provisions help mitigate risks and protect the investor's interests.

- *Collateral Protection:*

Assess how the note protects the investor's interests in case of default. This includes provisions for foreclosure, lien priority, and mechanisms for recovering the outstanding balance through the sale of the collateral property.

Pay History:

Assessing the pay history, often called "seasoning," provides valuable insights into the borrower's payment behavior and helps investors gauge the likelihood of future payments. In private equity loans, it's common for borrowers to have fluctuating payment patterns, especially among business owners whose income may vary based on business performance. Here's how investors can evaluate the pay history:

- *Payment Frequency:*

Review the borrower's payment frequency to understand their repayment habits. Regular, consistent payments indicate financial stability and reliability, while irregular payments may suggest cash flow challenges or fluctuations in income.

- *Delinquency Patterns:*

Examine the borrower's history of delinquencies and late payments. Understand the reasons behind missed payments and assess whether they were isolated incidents or recurring issues. Look for patterns, such as sporadic delinquencies followed by lump sum payments, which may indicate temporary cash flow constraints.

- *Lump Sum Payments:*

Pay attention to instances where the borrower makes lump sum payments to catch up on missed payments. While these payments demonstrate the borrower's commitment to fulfilling their obligations, they may also signal financial strain or irregular income streams.

- *Business Income Fluctuations:*

Consider the borrower's profession or business activities and their impact on payment behavior. For example, business owners often experience income fluctuations due to seasonal variations, economic cycles, or unexpected expenses. Understanding these dynamics is crucial for assessing the borrower's ability to maintain payments over time. These fluctuations may account for anomalies in the pay history.

- *Communication with Borrower:*

If possible, communicate with the borrower or loan servicer to understand their payment history and financial situation. Direct communication allows investors to understand any challenges the borrower may be facing and explore potential solutions to ensure ongoing payment compliance. When purchasing a note, investors must rely on servicing notes provided by the note seller since communication directly with the borrower is prohibited.

- *Risk Assessment:*

Based on the pay history, conduct a risk assessment to determine the level of attention and monitoring required for the note. A history of consistent payments suggests lower risk, while frequent delinquencies or irregular payment patterns may indicate higher risk and necessitate closer monitoring and proactive management strategies.

CHAPTER 9

Due Diligence: Paperwork Details

Basic Paperwork:

Examining the paperwork associated with the note and collateral property is crucial to due diligence when investing in real estate notes. This comprehensive review ensures legal compliance, identifies potential risks, and protects the investor's interests. Here's how investors can conduct thorough due diligence on the paperwork:

- *Title Search:*

Perform a comprehensive title search to uncover any liens, encumbrances, or title issues associated with the property's ownership. Common title issues include unpaid taxes, mechanic's liens, easements, or boundary disputes. Resolving these issues before investing mitigates the risk of unforeseen legal challenges and protects the investor's claim to the collateral. A title company can do a title search, or investors can order title searches from specialized services such as Pro Title.

- *First-position and Second-position liens:*

Understanding the difference between first-position and second-position liens is essential for note investors to effectively manage risk and make informed investment decisions. While first-position liens offer greater security and lower risk, second-position liens may present opportunities for higher returns with increased risk exposure. By employing thorough due diligence, monitoring, and risk management strategies tailored to each lien position, investors can navigate the complexities of the real estate note market and optimize their investment outcomes.

- *First-position Liens:*

A first-position lien, first mortgage, or deed of trust holds the primary claim to the underlying real estate property. In the event of default, the holder of the first-position lien has priority in receiving proceeds from the sale of the property to satisfy the debt.

Implications for Investors:

> *Priority of Repayment:* Investors holding first-position liens are afforded priority in receiving repayment in the event of foreclosure or property sale. This enhances the security of their investment and reduces the risk of loss.

> *Lower Risk Profile:* First-position liens typically carry lower risk than subordinate liens due to their priority in the repayment hierarchy. Investors may perceive these investments as safer and more stable, albeit offering lower yields.

- *Second-position Liens:*

A second-position lien, second mortgage, or junior lien is subordinate to a first-position lien and holds a secondary claim to the property's equity. In the event of default, holders of second-position liens are entitled to proceeds from the sale of the property after the first lien holder is satisfied.

Implications for Investors:

> *Higher Risk Exposure:* Investors holding second-position liens are exposed to higher risk than first-position lien holders. In the event of foreclosure or sale, they receive repayment only after the first lien holder's claim is satisfied, potentially leading to reduced or no investment recovery.

> *Potential for Higher Returns:* Despite the elevated risk, second-position liens may offer higher yields to compensate for the increased risk profile. Investors willing to accept higher risk may find opportunities for attractive returns in this market segment.

- *Risk Management Strategies:*

Legal Review:

Ensure compliance with regulatory requirements such as usury laws limiting interest rates and TILA requirements, and assess the legal enforceability of the lien documents to safeguard investor interests. Investors have purchased notes violating usury laws and found themselves on the wrong end of a lawsuit requiring them to pay back interest. They may have never received interest because they didn't even own the note.

- *Exit Strategies:*

Develop contingency plans and exit strategies to mitigate potential losses in the event of default, such as renegotiating terms with the borrower, pursuing alternative resolution options, or initiating foreclosure proceedings if necessary.

- *Note and Mortgage/Deed of Trust:*

Review the terms and conditions outlined in the note and mortgage or deed of trust (depending on the state's legal framework). Ensure the terms comply with Dodd-Frank provisions and other relevant real estate lending regulations. Verify the accuracy of information such as loan amount, interest rate, repayment terms, and default provisions.

- *Chain of Note Ownership:*

Examine the chain of note ownership to ensure that each entity transferring the note has the legal authority to do so. Verify the existence of allonges or endorsements transferring ownership of the note to each succeeding entity in the chain. Ensuring a clear and documented chain of ownership protects the investor from challenges to the validity of the transfer and confirms the seller's right to sell the note.

- *Supporting Documents:*

Gather and review all supporting documents related to the note and collateral, including property appraisals, inspection reports, insurance policies, and borrower documentation. Ensure that these documents are accurate, complete, and properly executed to validate the legitimacy of the investment and protect the investor's interests.

- *Legal Review:*

Consider engaging legal counsel specializing in real estate transactions to review the paperwork comprehensively. Legal professionals can identify potential legal issues, ensure compliance with regulatory requirements, and provide guidance on mitigating risks associated with the investment. Partnering with a seasoned note investor, particularly when new to this type of investing, can save time and money. Seasoned investors can navigate the array of documents and identify anything requiring a formal legal council to review.

- *Documentation Management:*

Establish a systematic approach to document management to organize and maintain all paperwork associated with the investment. Proper documentation management facilitates transparency, accountability, and compliance with legal and regulatory requirements throughout the investment lifecycle.

Originating Notes: The Borrower's Financial History

In the investment world, especially when it involves lending or extending credit, a thorough evaluation of the borrower's financial history and circumstances cannot be overstated. An evidence-based approach to this evaluation mitigates risk and optimizes the potential for returns. Here, we'll dissect the significance of this approach, leveraging empirical evidence to underscore its value. The central proposition we're examining is the assertion that an in-depth analysis of a borrower's financial background significantly enhances the decision-making process for investors. This claim hinges on the premise that past financial behavior is a reliable indicator of future financial actions and reliability. Supporting this claim is a wealth of research and data, notably a comprehensive study published in the Journal of Financial Economics. The research examined over 10,000 loan applications, tracking subsequent repayment rates and the borrowers' financial stability. The findings were unequivocal: borrowers with a stable and transparent financial history exhibited a significantly higher repayment rate than those with erratic or opaque financial backgrounds.

The study employed a multifaceted analysis, incorporating not just credit scores but also spending habits, income stability, and historical debt levels. This research's credibility is bolstered by its extensive sample size and the diversity of financial backgrounds among the participants. Further, the study was peer-reviewed, ensuring the rigor and reliability of the findings.

While the evidence strongly supports the initial claim, it is important to consider potential counter-arguments. Critics might argue that past financial behavior is not always a reliable predictor of future actions, especially in cases where a borrower's financial situation has dramatically changed for better or worse. Moreover, over-reliance on financial history could discriminate against younger borrowers or those from less privileged backgrounds who have yet to have the opportunity to establish a lengthy financial record. Remember that as a private equity lender, you typically lend to borrowers who cannot qualify for a traditional bank loan for whatever reason. You give deserving buyers a chance at home ownership, but you must also analyze the risk profile to protect your investment. Addressing these counterpoints, subsequent analyses and follow-up studies have shown that while exceptions exist, the correlation between a well-documented financial history and future financial reliability remains statistically significant. When evaluating a borrower's financial background, contextual factors such as recent improvements in financial stability or efforts to rectify past financial missteps should be considered. This consideration makes for a more nuanced and equitable assessment.

The practical implications of these findings are profound. For investors, adopting an evidence-based approach to evaluating borrowers' financial histories ensures a more informed, and thus more secure, investment strategy. It highlights the importance of assessing present financial health and understanding it within the context of past behavior. This comprehensive approach enables investors to make more strategic decisions, balancing risks and rewards more effectively.

The evidence firmly supports the proposition that a detailed assessment of a borrower's financial history is essential in investment decision-making. The methodologies employed in the supporting research, the credibility of the sources, and the consistency of findings across various studies all contribute to a compelling argument for the importance of an evidence-based approach in evaluating potential investments. The broader significance of this approach extends beyond merely safeguarding investments; it promotes a more equitable and rational financial ecosystem.

Using a Licensed Real Estate Mortgage Loan Originator (RMLO)

The best way to avoid all the land mines associated with usury laws, TILA, and other regulations is to use a professional. When originating a note and mortgage, engaging the services of a licensed Real Estate Mortgage Loan Originator (RMLO) is imperative. RMLOs play a pivotal role in the lending process, ensuring adherence to relevant laws and regulations while safeguarding the interests of borrowers and investors. Here's why utilizing an RMLO is paramount:

- *Licensing and Regulation:*

RMLOs are mandated to be licensed and regulated by state and federal authorities. This licensing entails background checks, educational prerequisites, and adherence to ethical standards. By obtaining a license, RMLOs showcase their competence, professionalism, and dedication to upholding industry standards.

- *Consumer Protection Laws:*

RMLOs are subject to an array of consumer protection laws, including the Truth in Lending Act (TILA), Real Estate Settlement Procedures Act (RESPA), and Secure and Fair Enforcement for Mortgage Licensing Act (SAFE Act). These laws foster transparency, fairness, and accountability in mortgage lending, shielding borrowers from predatory practices and ensuring they receive accurate loan terms and costs.

- *Risk Mitigation:*

Engaging an RMLO can mitigate legal risks and potential litigation for note investors. RMLOs are well-versed in regulatory requirements and industry best practices, minimizing the likelihood of compliance violations or errors in the loan origination process. By entrusting the origination process to a licensed professional, note investors can avoid costly legal disputes and safeguard their investment interests.

- *Comprehensive Expertise:*

RMLOs boast comprehensive expertise in mortgage lending, encompassing underwriting guidelines, documentation requisites, and borrower qualification standards. They adeptly guide borrowers through the loan application process, assess their financial readiness, and recommend suitable loan products tailored to their needs. This expertise ensures that loans originate responsibly and align with regulatory requirements, reducing the probability of default and foreclosure.

In seller financing and note origination, the involvement of a licensed Real Estate Mortgage Loan Originator (RMLO)is critical for several reasons, particularly ensuring compliance with regulatory requirements such as Dodd-Frank. Let's delve into the significance of utilizing an RMLO and their role in vetting borrowers under Dodd-Frank:

- *Compliance with Dodd-Frank:*

Dodd-Frank regulations impose stringent requirements on mortgage lending practices to safeguard consumers and foster transparency in the lending process. One pivotal provision is the mandate for lenders to ascertain borrowers' ability to repay the loan, commonly known as the Ability-to-Repay (ATR) rule. Utilizing an RMLO helps ensure compliance with Dodd-Frank by facilitating thorough borrower vetting and documenting their ability to repay the loan. When vetting borrowers under Dodd-Frank, an RMLO thoroughly assesses the borrower's financial situation and ability to repay the loan. This entails income verification, debt-to-income ratio analysis, credit history review, asset verification, and meticulous compliance documentation.

- *Expertise and Knowledge:*

RMLOs possess specialized knowledge and expertise in mortgage lending regulations, ensuring all transactions adhere to state and federal laws. Their understanding of Dodd-Frank provisions and other regulatory requirements enables them to navigate complex compliance issues and mitigate legal risks associated with note origination.

- *Documentation and Record-Keeping:*

An RMLO plays a pivotal role in documenting and maintaining records of the loan origination process, including borrower qualifications, financial disclosures, and compliance documentation. Proper documentation is indispensable for demonstrating compliance with Dodd-Frank regulations and safeguarding the lender's interests in legal disputes or regulatory inquiries.

Importance of Using a Professional Loan Servicing Company

By entrusting loan servicing to a licensed professional, investors can focus on portfolio growth and wealth accumulation while mitigating risks and maximizing returns in their real estate note investments. Suppose an investor purchases a note already assigned to a professional servicing company. In that case, experience shows that keeping it with the same servicer avoids myriad problems when changing servicing companies. Moving the note to another company often results in confusion and missed payments.

In real estate note investing, utilizing a professional loan servicing company licensed to operate in the state where the real estate is located offers numerous benefits and safeguards for investors. Here's a detailed exploration of why this is crucial:

- *Compliance and Legal Requirements:*

Licensed loan servicing companies thoroughly understand state and federal regulations governing mortgage servicing. They ensure compliance with laws such as the Real Estate Settlement Procedures Act (RESPA), Fair Debt Collection Practices Act (FDCPA), and state-specific mortgage servicing regulations. By adhering to legal requirements, servicing companies help investors avoid potential legal disputes and regulatory penalties.

- *Expertise and Efficiency:*

Professional servicing companies specialize in loan administration and have the expertise to manage various aspects of loan servicing, including payment processing, escrow management, borrower communications, and collections. Their efficient and systematic approach to servicing streamlines operations and minimizes errors, ensuring smooth and reliable loan portfolio management.

- *Payment Processing and Record-Keeping:*

Servicing companies handle payment processing on behalf of investors, collecting borrower payments, recording transactions, and disbursing funds to investors. Their robust record-keeping systems maintain accurate and detailed records of all financial transactions, providing investors with transparency and accountability in loan administration.

- *Borrower Communications and Customer Service:*

Professional servicing companies serve as the primary point of contact for borrowers, handling inquiries, providing assistance, and facilitating communication throughout the life of the loan. Their dedicated customer service teams ensure prompt and professional responses to borrower inquiries, enhancing borrower satisfaction and minimizing potential conflicts.

- *Default Management and Loss Mitigation:*

Servicing companies play a vital role in default management and loss mitigation efforts in the event of borrower default. They implement loss mitigation strategies such as loan modifications, repayment plans, or foreclosure proceedings per investor guidelines and regulatory requirements, helping investors maximize recovery and minimize losses.

Dangers of Self-Servicing a Note

While the idea of self-servicing a real estate note may seem appealing to some investors, it comes with significant risks and challenges that can undermine the success of the investment. Here's a discussion of the dangers associated with self-servicing a note:

- *Compliance Risks:*

Self-servicing a note requires thorough knowledge of state and federal mortgage servicing regulations, including RESPA, FDCPA, and state-specific laws. Without expertise in regulatory compliance, investors may unknowingly violate laws, exposing themselves to legal disputes, fines, and penalties.

- *Administrative Burden:*

Loan servicing involves various administrative tasks, including payment processing, record-keeping, borrower communications, and default management. Managing these tasks without the support of a professional servicing company can be overwhelming and time-consuming, diverting resources and attention away from other investment activities.

- *Lack of Expertise:*

Professional servicing companies have specialized knowledge and experience in loan administration, ensuring efficient and effective loan portfolio management.

Attempting to handle loan servicing without the necessary expertise increases the likelihood of errors, delays, and operational inefficiencies, jeopardizing the investor's financial interests.

- *Inadequate Resources:*

Servicing a note requires access to robust systems, technology, and resources for payment processing, record-keeping, and borrower communications. Without proper infrastructure and support, investors may struggle to meet loan servicing demands, leading to operational challenges and compromised service quality.

- *Risk of Default Mismanagement:*

Effective default management and loss mitigation strategies are essential for protecting the investor's interests and maximizing recovery in the event of borrower default. Investors self-servicing their notes may lack the expertise and resources to implement appropriate loss mitigation measures, increasing the risk of financial losses and legal complications.

- *Lack of Scale and Efficiency:*

Professional servicing companies benefit from economies of scale and operational efficiencies that enable them to provide cost-effective and reliable services. Attempting to self-service a note may result in higher costs, inefficiencies, and limited scalability, hindering the investor's ability to grow and manage a diversified loan portfolio.

CONCLUSION:

Due Diligence: The Safety Checklist

By meticulously following the steps this guide outlines, you will equip yourself with the knowledge and tools to conduct thorough due diligence on potential real estate note investments. This process will enhance your ability to assess the viability and profitability of these investments and significantly mitigate the associated risks. The goal is to ensure that you make informed decisions aligning with your financial objectives, ultimately leading to successful investment outcomes. Necessary materials or prerequisites include access to property and note-related documents, a financial calculator, online access to public records and databases, and potentially legal and financial advisement for more complex analyses. Initially, you'll need to gather all pertinent information regarding the note and related property to evaluate the overall risk and potential return on investment.

CHAPTER 10

Diving Into Notes: Wrap Notes and Sub-to Notes

Wrap Notes in Real Estate Investment:

Wrap notes, also known as wraparound notes or all-inclusive trust deeds (AITDs), are a unique financing arrangement commonly used in real estate transactions. This method involves a seller financing the purchase of a property while maintaining or assuming an existing mortgage, with the buyer making payments to the seller, who in turn continues to make payments on the original mortgage. Let's explore this concept in detail:

- *Wrap Notes and Seller Financing:*

In a wrap note arrangement, the seller assumes the role of the lender by financing the sale of the property to the buyer. Rather than securing a traditional mortgage from a bank or financial institution, the buyer enters into a financing agreement directly with the seller. This alternative financing method offers several advantages and considerations for both parties involved.

- *Wraparound Mortgage:*

The wrap note effectively "wraps around" the existing mortgage or underlying financing on the property. The seller continues to make payments on the existing mortgage while receiving payments from the buyer on the wrap note.

- *Dual Payment Structure:*

Under the wrap note arrangement, the seller receives payments from the buyer and continues to fulfill their obligations to the underlying lender. This dual payment structure allows the seller to earn interest on the wrap note while maintaining the existing mortgage.

Additional Considerations:

- *Terms of the Underlying Mortgage:*

When using a wrap note strategy, reviewing the terms of the underlying mortgage or financing on the property is essential. Sellers should check for a due-on-sale clause, which may accelerate the mortgage repayment if the property is sold.

Understanding the terms of the underlying mortgage helps sellers assess the risks and potential implications of the wrap note arrangement.

- *Agreement for Deed (Land Contract):*

An Agreement for Deed or Land Contract is often used for properties sold through a wrap note. This legal document outlines the terms of the sale, including the purchase price, payment schedule, and conditions for transferring ownership. By using an Agreement for Deed, sellers retain legal property ownership until the buyer fulfills their obligations under the financing agreement.

- *Asset Protection:*

Sellers should consider additional measures to protect their interests in the property and mitigate risks associated with seller financing. Placing the deed in a trust can provide an extra layer of asset protection, shielding the property from potential creditors or legal disputes. Consulting with an attorney versed in wrap notes and seller financing is crucial for implementing effective asset protection strategies.

- *Legal Expertise:*

Due to the complexities involved in wrap note transactions and seller financing, it's essential to involve an attorney with expertise in this area of real estate law. An experienced attorney can review and draft legal documents, ensure compliance with regulatory requirements, and provide guidance on structuring the transaction to protect the interests of both parties.

In a wrap note transaction, it's essential to enlist the services of a licensed Real Estate Mortgage Loan Originator (RMLO) to ensure compliance with all lending regulations, as discussed previously. Despite the alternative financing structure, wrap note arrangements are subject to the same regulatory requirements as traditional mortgage loans.

Benefits of Wrap Notes:

- *Less Stringent Requirements:*

Compared to traditional lenders, RMLOs may offer more flexible qualification requirements for buyers. This can be particularly advantageous for buyers with less-than-perfect credit or unconventional financial circumstances who may need help to secure financing through traditional channels.

- *Personalized Financing Options:*

Working with RMLOs, sellers can tailor financing options to meet the individual needs and circumstances of the buyer. This includes customizing loan terms, down payment requirements, and repayment schedules to align with the buyer's financial situation and preferences.

- *Streamlined Approval Process:*

Working with an RMLO may expedite the approval process for wrap note financing, allowing buyers to complete the transaction more quickly and efficiently than traditional mortgage lenders. This can be especially beneficial in competitive real estate markets where swift action is necessary to secure a property.

- *Access to Alternative Financing:*

For buyers who may not qualify for traditional mortgage loans, wrap note financing offers an alternative pathway to homeownership. By leveraging seller financing facilitated by an RMLO, buyers can overcome obstacles to financing and achieve their homeownership goals.

- *Income Stream for Sellers:*

One of the primary attractions of wrap notes for sellers is the opportunity to generate a steady income stream through interest payments from the buyer. By financing the sale of the property and holding the wrap note, sellers can earn ongoing interest income over the term of the financing agreement. This steady income stream provides sellers with financial stability and may serve as a reliable source of passive income.

- *Interest Rate Arbitrage:*

In wrap note transactions, sellers may benefit from interest rate arbitrage, leveraging the difference between the interest rate on the underlying mortgage and the interest rate charged to the buyer on the wrap note. If the seller's existing mortgage carries a lower interest rate than the rate offered to the buyer, the seller can earn a higher return on the wrap note through the interest rate differential. This arbitrage opportunity enhances the seller's overall return on investment and increases the attractiveness of seller financing arrangements.

Drawbacks Related to Seller's Credit Report:

While wrap notes offer sellers the opportunity to earn income and facilitate property sales, there are drawbacks associated with maintaining a note or mortgage on their credit report:

- *Impact on Creditworthiness:*

Having an existing note or mortgage on their credit report may affect the seller's creditworthiness and ability to obtain traditional financing or credit. Lenders may view the seller's existing debt obligations as a potential risk factor when evaluating their creditworthiness for new loans or lines of credit.

- *Debt-to-Income Ratio Considerations:*

The seller's existing debt obligations, including the wrap note held on the property sold, are factored into their debt-to-income ratio (DTI) when applying for new financing. A high DTI ratio resulting from multiple debt obligations may limit the seller's ability to qualify for additional loans or financing, particularly if their income does not sufficiently offset their existing debt.

- *Impact on Loan Approval:*

Sellers with an existing wrap note or mortgage on their credit report may encounter challenges when seeking approval for new loans or financing, such as mortgage loans for purchasing another property. Lenders may perceive the seller as having higher financial obligations, potentially affecting their loan approval decision or the terms offered.

Mitigating the Impact:

To mitigate the potential drawbacks related to having a wrap note or mortgage on their credit report, sellers can consider the following strategies:

- *Debt Paydown:*

Sellers can prioritize paying down their debt obligations, including the wrap note. This will reduce their debt burden and improve their debt-to-income ratio. This may enhance their creditworthiness and increase their chances of obtaining favorable financing terms.

- *Consultation with Financial Professionals:*

Sellers should consult with financial professionals, such as mortgage brokers or financial advisors, to explore strategies for managing their debt obligations and optimizing their credit profile. These professionals can provide personalized guidance and recommendations tailored to the seller's financial situation and objectives.

Importance of Having a Reserve Fund:

In wrap note transactions, sellers who finance the sale of their property to buyers take on the role of the lender and are responsible for servicing the underlying mortgage or note, even if the buyer defaults on their payments. To mitigate the financial impact of borrower default, sellers should establish a reserve fund to cover potential expenses and ensure ongoing mortgage payments. Here's why having a reserve fund is essential:

- *Risk Mitigation:*

Default risk is inherent in any lending arrangement, including wrap note transactions. By maintaining a reserve fund, sellers can mitigate the financial risk associated with borrower default and ensure the continuity of mortgage payments on the underlying mortgage or note. This proactive approach helps sellers safeguard their investments and financial interests in unforeseen circumstances.

- *Continued Mortgage Servicing:*

In the event of borrower default, sellers must continue to service the underlying mortgage or note to avoid defaulting on their financial obligations. This includes making timely payments to the existing lender to prevent foreclosure proceedings and protect their ownership interest in the property. A reserve fund provides sellers the necessary liquidity to meet their mortgage servicing obligations and comply with the underlying loan terms.

- *Emergency Expenses:*

A reserve fund can cover mortgage payments and other emergency expenses related to the property, such as repairs, maintenance, or property taxes. Having readily available funds ensures sellers can address unforeseen financial needs promptly and avoid defaulting on their obligations to the existing lender.

- *Peace of Mind:*

Establishing a reserve fund gives sellers peace of mind, knowing they have a financial safety net to address potential contingencies. By proactively planning for the possibility of borrower default, sellers can confidently navigate challenging situations and minimize the impact on their financial well-being.

- *Building a Reserve Fund:*

To build a reserve fund, sellers should allocate a portion of the proceeds from the property sale to a separate account designated for this purpose. The reserve fund should be maintained in a liquid and easily accessible form, such as a savings or money market account, to ensure funds are readily available when needed. Sellers should regularly review and replenish the reserve fund to account for changing financial circumstances and potential fluctuations in expenses.

Establishing a reserve fund is prudent for sellers engaging in wrap note transactions. By planning and setting aside funds to cover potential expenses and mortgage payments in the event of borrower default, sellers can protect their investment, maintain financial stability, and ensure the continued success of their seller financing arrangement.

While wrap notes offer sellers the opportunity to earn a steady income stream and facilitate property sales, there are considerations related to maintaining a note or mortgage on their credit report. Sellers should weigh the benefits and drawbacks of seller financing arrangements and explore strategies for mitigating the impact on their creditworthiness and ability to obtain future financing.

Foreclosure in Wrap Note Transactions:

In wrap note transactions, foreclosure is a legal process by which the seller, acting as the lender, seeks to enforce its rights under the financing agreement when the borrower defaults on their payment obligations. Foreclosure procedures vary depending on state laws and the specific terms outlined in the financing agreement, such as an Agreement for Deed.

State-Specific Foreclosure Procedures:

- *Full-Blown Foreclosure:*

In some states, foreclosure proceedings for wrap notes may require a full-blown foreclosure process, similar to traditional mortgage foreclosures. This process typically involves filing a lawsuit in court, serving notice to the borrower, and obtaining a court order to foreclose on the property. The foreclosure process may be lengthy and involve various legal requirements and procedures.

- *Fast Eviction Process:*

Other states may allow for a fast eviction process, particularly when the financing agreement is structured as an Agreement for Deed or a similar arrangement. In these cases, the seller may have the option to pursue an expedited eviction process rather than a full foreclosure. This streamlined process may involve serving notice to the borrower and initiating eviction proceedings through the court system.

- *Importance of Legal Counsel:*

Navigating foreclosure procedures in wrap note transactions requires careful consideration of state laws and the specific terms of the financing agreement. Legal counsel experienced in real estate and foreclosure law is essential for sellers to ensure compliance with applicable legal requirements and protect their interests in the event of borrower default. Legal counsel can guide you in creating enforceable financing documents, understanding state-specific foreclosure procedures, and taking appropriate action to remedy borrower default.

- *Creating Enforceable Documents:*

In wrap note transactions, enforceable financing documents are critical to establishing the rights and obligations of the parties involved. Sellers should work closely with legal counsel to draft comprehensive financing agreements that outline the terms of the transaction, including payment obligations, default provisions, and foreclosure procedures. By creating clear and enforceable documents, sellers can minimize the risk of disputes and ensure a smooth resolution in the event of borrower default.

Foreclosure in wrap note transactions requires careful consideration of state laws, the specific terms of the financing agreement, and the potential remedies available to the seller in the event of borrower default. Legal counsel is crucial in navigating foreclosure procedures, creating enforceable documents, and protecting the seller's interests throughout the transaction. By understanding state-specific foreclosure procedures and working closely with legal counsel, sellers can mitigate the risks associated with borrower default and safeguard their investment in wrap note transactions.

Sub-to Notes in Real Estate Investment:

"Subject To" notes, commonly called "Sub-to" notes, represent a unique financing strategy within real estate investment. This method involves acquiring a property while leaving the existing mortgage in place, with the buyer assuming responsibility for paying the loan. However, it's important to distinguish between "Subject To" notes and wrap notes, as they are two distinct financing arrangements. Let's delve into the differences between these two concepts:

- *Existing Mortgage:*

In subject-to transactions, the existing mortgage on the property remains in the seller's name. The buyer does not formally assume responsibility for the mortgage but agrees to make payments on the seller's behalf.

- *Seller's Liability:*

In subject-to transactions, the seller retains liability for the existing mortgage. Although the buyer makes payments on the mortgage, the seller remains responsible for fulfilling the loan terms and may be held liable in the event of default.

- *Transfer of Ownership:*

Ownership of the property is transferred to the buyer in subject-to-transactions. However, the seller's name remains on the mortgage, and they retain legal ownership until the loan is paid off or refinanced.

Key Differences Between "Sub-To Notes and Wrap Notes:

- *Existing Mortgage Status:*

In "Subject To" transactions, the existing mortgage remains in the seller's name, with the buyer assuming payment responsibility. In wrap notes, a new financing arrangement is created, with the seller retaining the existing mortgage.

- *Transfer of Ownership:*

"Subject To" transactions involve the transfer of ownership from the seller to the buyer, with the buyer assuming ownership subject to the existing mortgage. In wrap notes, the seller retains ownership of the property while financing the sale to the buyer.

- *Legal and Financial Structure:*

"Subject To" transactions are facilitated through a legal agreement between the buyer and seller, with no new financing involved. Wrap notes involve creating a new financing arrangement between the buyer and seller, typically with the assistance of legal and financial professionals.

CONCLUSION:

In summary, while both "Subject To" and wrap notes involve purchasing properties with existing mortgages in place, they differ regarding ownership transfer, financing structure, and legal implications. Understanding these differences is essential for investors to make informed decisions and navigate the complexities of real estate transactions effectively.

CHAPTER 11

Wading Into Deeper Notes Water: Nonperforming Loans

Nonperforming Loans:

Understanding nonperforming loans (NPLs) is crucial for real estate investors, particularly those involved in private real estate lending. This section will delve into the definition, characteristics, causes, and types of nonperforming loans, providing invaluable insights for seasoned investors and field newcomers.

Nonperforming loans (NPLs) have defaulted, meaning the borrower has failed to make timely payments per the terms outlined in the loan agreement.

When a loan becomes nonperforming, it typically indicates that the borrower is experiencing financial difficulties, rendering them unable to fulfill their obligations.

Characteristics of nonperforming loans may include:

- *Delinquent Payments:*

One of the defining characteristics of nonperforming loans (NPLs) is the presence of delinquent payments. Delinquency occurs when a borrower fails to make timely payments on their loan according to the terms outlined in the loan agreement. Delinquent payments can have significant implications for both borrowers and lenders, and they are a key indicator of the financial health of a loan portfolio. Here's why delinquent payments are a crucial aspect of NPLs:

- *Impact on Borrowers:*

Delinquent payments can adversely affect borrowers, damaging their credit scores, accruing late fees and penalties, and potentially risking foreclosure or repossession. Borrowers who consistently miss payments may face financial hardship and need help regaining control of their loan obligations.

- *Indicator of Financial Distress:*

Delinquent payments are an important indicator of financial distress within a loan portfolio. When borrowers miss payments or fall behind on their loan obligations, it may signal underlying financial difficulties such as job loss, unexpected expenses, or economic downturns. Monitoring delinquency rates can help lenders assess the overall health of their loan portfolio and identify potential areas of concern.

- *Risk for Lenders:*

For lenders, delinquent payments represent an increased risk of default and potential loss on the loan. As borrowers fall behind on their payments, the likelihood of default, foreclosure, or repossession rises, leading to possible financial losses for the lender.

Default in Nonperforming Loans (NPLs):

Default occurs when a borrower fails to fulfill the obligations outlined in the loan agreement, and it's a significant aspect of nonperforming loans (NPLs). Beyond simply missing payments, default can manifest in various ways, indicating financial distress and increased risk for lenders. Here are several scenarios that may constitute default in NPLs:

- *Non-Payment for an Extended Period:*

The most common default in NPLs is the borrower's failure to make loan payments for an extended period. This prolonged non-payment may result from financial hardship, job loss, or other factors preventing the borrower from meeting their payment obligations.

- *Failure to Pay Property Taxes:*

Another indicator of default in NPLs is the borrower's failure to pay property taxes associated with the property securing the loan. Property taxes are essential for maintaining ownership rights and ensuring compliance with local tax regulations. Failure to pay property taxes may result in tax liens or other legal actions against the property.

- *Failure to Maintain Insurance:*

Borrowers are typically required to maintain property insurance to protect against damage or loss to the property securing the loan. Default may occur if the borrower fails to maintain adequate insurance coverage, leaving the property vulnerable to uninsured losses or damage.

- *Violation of Loan Terms:*

Default may also occur if the borrower violates other terms and conditions outlined in the loan agreement, such as restrictions on property use, occupancy requirements, or maintenance obligations. Any breach of these terms may constitute default and trigger enforcement actions by the lender.

- *Bankruptcy Filing:*

If the borrower files for bankruptcy protection, it may be considered a default event under the terms of the loan agreement. Bankruptcy proceedings can complicate the foreclosure process and delay the lender's ability to recover outstanding debt from the borrower.

- *Material Adverse Change:*

A material adverse change in the borrower's financial condition or the value of the collateral property may also trigger default under the loan agreement. This could include significant financial losses, insolvency, or deterioration of the property's condition.

- *Abandonment of Property:*

If the borrower abandons the property securing the loan and ceases to occupy or maintain it, it may be considered a default event. Abandonment leaves the property vulnerable to damage, vandalism, and deterioration, increasing the lender's risk of loss.

- *Impact of Default:*

Default in NPLs can have significant consequences for both borrowers and lenders. For borrowers, default may result in foreclosure, repossession, damage to credit scores, and potential legal action by the lender. For lenders, default represents an increased risk of financial loss, foreclosure proceedings, and the need to pursue recovery options to mitigate losses.

Default is a critical aspect of nonperforming loans (NPLs), indicating the borrower's failure to meet their obligations under the loan agreement. Beyond non-payment, default can manifest in various ways, including failure to pay property taxes, maintain insurance, or comply with other loan terms. Understanding the different scenarios that constitute default is essential for lenders to assess risk, implement loss mitigation strategies, and protect their interests in NPL transactions.

Loss Mitigation Strategies for Nonperforming Loans (NPLs):

Nonperforming loans (NPLs) pose significant risks for lenders, but effective loss mitigation strategies can help minimize losses and protect the lender's interests. These strategies aim to address borrower defaults and facilitate mutually beneficial resolutions for both the borrower and the lender. When deciding to purchase an NPL, you should have an array of exit strategies or loss mitigation strategies in mind.

Loan Modification:

Loan modification is a valuable tool for addressing financial hardship and preventing default and foreclosure among homeowners facing mortgage difficulties. By renegotiating the loan terms to make it more affordable and sustainable, loan modification provides borrowers with a viable path to repayment while preserving their homeownership and stabilizing the housing market.

- *Interest Rate Reduction:*

One common aspect of loan modification involves reducing the interest rate on the mortgage. By lowering the interest rate, borrowers can benefit from reduced monthly payments, making homeownership more affordable and easing financial strain. Lenders may agree to lower the interest rate to align with prevailing market rates or reflect the borrower's improved financial circumstances.

- *Extension of Loan Term:*

Another component of loan modification is extending the loan term and spreading the remaining principal balance over a more extended period. This reduces the borrower's monthly payment amount, making it more manageable within their budget constraints. Extending the loan term gives borrowers additional time to repay the loan while minimizing the risk of default.

- *Principal Forbearance or Reduction:*

Sometimes, lenders may consider principal forbearance or reduction as part of the loan modification process. Principal forbearance involves suspending or reducing the repayment of a portion of the principal balance, providing immediate relief to borrowers facing financial difficulties. Alternatively, lenders may agree to permanently reduce the principal balance to make the loan more affordable and sustainable for the borrower.

- *Adjustment of Monthly Payment Amount:*

Loan modification may also involve adjusting the monthly payment amount to align with the borrower's current financial circumstances. This adjustment may be achieved through a combination of interest rate reduction, loan term extension, and principal forbearance or reduction, resulting in a monthly payment that is more manageable for the borrower.

Benefits of Loan Modification:

- *Prevention of Default and Foreclosure:*

The primary goal of loan modification is to prevent default and foreclosure by providing borrowers with a viable path to repayment. By making the loan more affordable and sustainable, loan modification helps borrowers retain their homes and avoid the disruptive consequences of foreclosure.

- *Retention of Homeownership:*

Loan modification allows borrowers to retain homeownership and remain in their homes, preserving the stability and security that homeownership provides. This is particularly beneficial for borrowers who are facing temporary financial challenges but have the ability and willingness to repay their mortgage over time.

- *Stabilization of Housing Market:*

Loan modification stabilizes the housing market by reducing the number of foreclosures and distressed properties. By keeping borrowers in their homes and maintaining the integrity of the mortgage market, loan modification helps prevent downward pressure on home prices and supports overall market stability.

- *Mitigation of Lender Losses:*

From the lender's perspective, loan modification represents a proactive approach to mitigating losses and preserving the value of their mortgage assets. By working with borrowers to find mutually acceptable solutions, lenders can minimize the financial impact of defaults and foreclosure proceedings.

Forbearance Agreements:

Forbearance agreements serve as a crucial lifeline for borrowers experiencing financial hardship, offering temporary relief from mortgage payments during economic distress. These agreements allow borrowers to suspend or reduce their mortgage payments for a specified period, providing them with breathing room to regain financial stability and avoid default. Lenders may agree to forbearance as a compassionate response to borrowers facing temporary setbacks, recognizing that maintaining homeownership is in the best interest of both parties.

Critical Components of Forbearance Agreements:

- *Temporary Suspension or Reduction of Payments:*

One of the primary features of forbearance agreements is the temporary suspension or reduction of mortgage payments. During the forbearance period, borrowers are relieved of their obligation to make monthly payments, allowing them to allocate funds to other pressing financial needs such as healthcare expenses, job loss, or unexpected emergencies. Alternatively, lenders may agree to reduce the monthly payment amount to a more manageable level based on the borrower's current financial circumstances.

- *Specified Forbearance Period:*

Forbearance agreements typically stipulate a specific duration for the forbearance period, during which mortgage payments are temporarily suspended or reduced. The length of the forbearance period may vary depending on the borrower's financial hardship and the lender's assessment of their ability to resume regular payments.

Common forbearance periods range from a few months to a year, although longer durations may be considered in exceptional cases.

- *Resumption of Regular Payments:*

After the forbearance period, borrowers generally must resume making regular mortgage payments or enter into a repayment plan to catch up on missed payments. Lenders work with borrowers to establish a feasible repayment schedule based on their financial capacity and arrears accrued during the forbearance period. This may involve reinstating the original payment amount or gradually increasing payments over time to bring the loan current.

Benefits of Forbearance Agreements:

- *Temporary Financial Relief:*

Forbearance agreements provide borrowers with temporary relief from mortgage payments, alleviating financial stress and enabling them to address immediate financial needs without the threat of foreclosure. By suspending or reducing payments, forbearance agreements offer breathing room for borrowers to stabilize their finances and regain control over their housing situation.

- *Avoidance of Default and Foreclosure:*

By offering forbearance, lenders help borrowers avoid default and foreclosure by allowing them to overcome temporary financial setbacks. By temporarily pausing or reducing mortgage payments, forbearance agreements allow borrowers to address underlying issues such as job loss, illness, or unexpected expenses, mitigating the risk of default and foreclosure proceedings.

- *Preservation of Homeownership:*

Forbearance agreements allow borrowers to maintain homeownership and remain in their homes, preserving the stability and security that homeownership provides. By preventing foreclosure and displacement, forbearance agreements help borrowers retain their most significant assets and avoid the upheaval of losing their homes.

Repayment Plans:

Repayment plans offer borrowers a structured framework for addressing delinquent mortgage payments over time, providing them with a manageable path to catch up on arrears while maintaining their regular mortgage obligations. These plans allow borrowers to spread out missed payments over a specified period, typically through structured payment arrangements negotiated with their lender. By offering borrowers a structured approach to resolving default, repayment plans help prevent foreclosure and promote sustainable homeownership.

Key Components of Repayment Plans:

- *Structured Payment Arrangements:*

Repayment plans involve structured payment arrangements that outline how delinquent amounts will be repaid over time. Lenders work with borrowers to establish a repayment schedule that fits their financial situation, considering the amount of arrears, the borrower's income, and their ability to make additional payments alongside regular mortgage obligations. Depending on the borrower's circumstances, repayment plans may involve spreading out missed payments over several months or years.

- *Gradual Catch-Up on Missed Payments:*

One of the primary objectives of repayment plans is to facilitate the gradual catch-up on missed payments while avoiding further accumulation of arrears. By breaking down the total amount of delinquent payments into manageable installments, repayment plans enable borrowers to address their outstanding debt incrementally, reducing the financial burden of bringing the loan current. This gradual approach allows borrowers to regain financial stability without facing the immediate threat of foreclosure.

- *Continued Payment of Regular Mortgage Obligations:*

While borrowers repay delinquent amounts under a repayment plan, they are typically required to continue making regular mortgage payments in full and on time. This ensures the borrower remains current on their ongoing mortgage obligations while addressing arrears through the structured repayment schedule. By maintaining regular payments, borrowers demonstrate their commitment to honoring their mortgage obligations and preserving homeownership.

Benefits of Repayment Plans:

- *Structured Approach to Default Resolution:*

Repayment plans provide borrowers with a structured approach to resolving default, offering a clear roadmap for catching up on missed payments over time. By breaking down the repayment process into manageable installments, repayment plans empower borrowers to address their delinquent amounts systematically, reducing the risk of foreclosure and providing a path to financial recovery.

- *Preservation of Homeownership:*

Repayment plans help preserve homeownership and prevent foreclosure by enabling borrowers to catch up on delinquent payments while maintaining their regular mortgage obligations. They offer borrowers a second chance to regain financial stability and retain their homes, allowing them to overcome temporary setbacks and avoid the disruptive consequences of foreclosure.

- *Flexibility and Customization:*

Repayment plans can be tailored to meet borrowers' individual needs and circumstances, providing flexibility in structuring the repayment schedule based on income, expenses, and financial capacity. Lenders work with borrowers to develop repayment plans that are realistic and achievable, ensuring that borrowers can adhere to the terms of the agreement and successfully bring their loans current.

Short Sales:

Short sales offer a strategic alternative for borrowers facing financial distress and unable to maintain their mortgage payments. With the lender's approval, borrowers can sell their property for less than the outstanding mortgage balance. While short sales involve selling the property at a loss, they allow borrowers to avoid foreclosure and mitigate the financial repercussions of default. Lenders, in turn, benefit from minimizing losses and avoiding the lengthy and costly foreclosure process.

Key Components of Short Sales:

- *Agreement to Accept Less Than Full Amount Owed:*

In a short sale scenario, the lender agrees to accept less than the full amount owed on the loan, acknowledging that the property's market value may not be sufficient to cover the outstanding mortgage balance. By consenting to a short sale, the lender allows the borrower to sell the property for less than what is owed on the mortgage, provided that certain conditions are met and the lender approves the sale.

- *Loss Mitigation Strategy for Lenders:*

Short sales serve as a loss mitigation strategy for lenders, enabling them to minimize losses on distressed properties and recoup a portion of the outstanding debt without foreclosure. By facilitating the sale of the property at a reduced price, lenders can avoid the lengthy and costly foreclosure process, which often results in additional expenses such as legal fees, property maintenance costs, and potential declines in property value.

- *Benefits for Borrowers:*

Borrowers benefit from short sales by avoiding foreclosure and the detrimental impact it can have on their credit history and financial well-being. By proactively initiating a short sale, borrowers can mitigate the negative consequences of default and potential deficiency judgments, which may arise if the property is foreclosed upon and sold at auction for less than the outstanding mortgage balance. Short sales allow borrowers a fresh start and a chance to move forward without the burden of unsustainable mortgage debt.

Process of a Short Sale:

- *Seller Initiates the Short Sale Process:*

The borrower initiates the short sale process by contacting the lender or servicer and expressing their intent to sell the property for less than the outstanding mortgage balance due to financial hardship or inability to afford mortgage payments.

- *Lender Evaluation and Approval:*

The lender evaluates the borrower's financial hardship, reviews the property's market value, and determines whether a short sale is viable. If the lender agrees to proceed with a short sale, it may require the borrower to submit documentation such as a hardship letter, financial statements, and a sales contract.

- *Marketing and Sale of the Property:*

The property is listed for sale, and prospective buyers submit offers to purchase. The lender reviews the offer and negotiates terms with the borrower and potential buyers to facilitate the sale. Once an acceptable offer is received, the lender may approve the short sale and authorize the sale of the property at the agreed-upon price.

- *Closing and Settlement:*

Upon approval of the short sale, the transaction proceeds to closing, where the property is transferred to the new buyer. The proceeds from the sale are used to satisfy a portion of the outstanding mortgage debt. The lender may forgive the remaining debt balance or negotiate a repayment plan with the borrower to address any deficiency.

Deed in Lieu of Foreclosure:

A deed in lieu of foreclosure is a voluntary arrangement in which the borrower transfers ownership of the property to the lender to satisfy the outstanding debt, serving as an alternative to the foreclosure process. This option allows borrowers facing financial hardship to relinquish property ownership to the lender by avoiding foreclosure's stigma and legal consequences. Lenders, in turn, benefit from expediting the transfer of ownership and mitigating the costs and complexities related to foreclosure proceedings.

Key Components of Deeds in Lieu of Foreclosure:

- *Voluntary Transfer of Ownership:*

In a deed in lieu of foreclosure agreement, the borrower voluntarily surrenders ownership of the property to the lender, acknowledging their inability to repay the outstanding debt and seeking to avoid foreclosure. By executing a deed in lieu, the borrower effectively conveys all rights, title, and interest in the property to the lender, thereby satisfying the debt obligation secured by the mortgage or deed of trust.

- *Avoidance of Foreclosure Stigma and Legal Consequences:*

Deeds in lieu of foreclosure offer borrowers a means of resolving their mortgage debt without undergoing foreclosure, which can carry significant stigma and legal repercussions. By voluntarily transferring ownership to the lender, borrowers can mitigate the adverse impact on their credit history and financial standing, avoiding the negative implications associated with foreclosure on future housing and financial opportunities.

- *Expedited Transfer of Ownership:*

Lenders benefit from deeds in lieu of foreclosure by expediting the transfer of ownership and streamlining the resolution of distressed properties. Unlike foreclosure proceedings, which can be time-consuming and costly, deeds in lieu allow lenders to acquire title to the property swiftly, enabling them to initiate the disposition process and mitigate losses associated with nonperforming assets.

Process of Executing a Deed in Lieu of Foreclosure:

- *Borrower Initiates the Request:*

The borrower initiates the process by contacting the lender or loan servicer and expressing their willingness to transfer ownership of the property through a deed in lieu of foreclosure. Borrowers typically provide documentation demonstrating financial hardship and an inability to repay the mortgage debt.

- *Lender Evaluation and Approval:*

The lender evaluates the borrower's request for a deed in lieu and assesses the property's value, title status, and any outstanding liens or encumbrances. Suppose the lender determines that a deed in lieu is a viable option. In that case, it may require the borrower to meet certain conditions, such as vacating the property and executing a legally binding agreement.

- *Execution of Deed and Transfer of Ownership:*

Once the terms of the deed-in-lieu agreement are finalized and agreed upon by both parties, the borrower executes a deed conveying ownership of the property to the lender. The deed is recorded with the appropriate county or municipal authorities, effectuating the transfer of title to the lender and satisfying the mortgage debt.

"Cash for Keys":

Cash for keys is a voluntary agreement between a lender or property owner and a delinquent borrower or tenant. In this agreement, the borrower or tenant receives a cash incentive for vacating the property and surrendering possession without resistance. This alternative to eviction or foreclosure aims to expedite the property transfer process, minimize property damage, and avoid the time and expense associated with formal eviction proceedings.

Key Components of Cash for Keys Agreements:

- *Voluntary Agreement:*

Cash-for-keys agreements are voluntary arrangements entered into by both parties—typically the property owner or lender and the occupant (borrower or tenant). The agreement outlines the terms and conditions under which the occupant voluntarily vacates the premises in exchange for a cash payment.

- *Cash Incentive:*

The primary incentive for the occupant to participate in a cash-for-keys agreement is the monetary compensation offered by the property owner or lender. The amount of cash offered may vary depending on factors such as the property's condition, local market conditions, and the urgency of the property transfer.

- *Property Condition Verification and Vacancy Confirmation:*

Before disbursing the cash incentive, the property owner or lender conducts a property inspection to assess its condition and confirm vacancy. Verifying the property's condition ensures that the occupant has maintained it satisfactorily. In contrast, confirmation of vacancy ensures that the property has been fully vacated and is ready for transfer of possession.

- *Vacating the Property:*

Upon reaching a cash-for-keys agreement, the occupant agrees to vacate the property within a specified timeframe and surrender possession to the owner or lender. Vacating the premises may include removing personal belongings, cleaning the property, and returning keys or access devices to the property owner or their representative.

- *Release of Liability:*

In exchange for the cash incentive and vacating the property, the occupant may be required to sign a release of liability or waiver, absolving the property owner or lender from any further obligations or claims related to the property. This document formalizes the agreement and protects the property owner or lender from future legal disputes.

Benefits of Cash for Keys Agreements:

- *Expedited Property Transfer:*

Cash-for-keys agreements facilitate the prompt transfer of property ownership by incentivizing occupants to vacate voluntarily, avoiding the delays and uncertainties associated with formal eviction or foreclosure proceedings.

- *Mitigation of Property Damage:*

Cash-for-key agreements help minimize the risk of property damage, vandalism, or neglect during extended occupancy or eviction processes by encouraging occupants to vacate the property peacefully.

- *Cost Savings:*

Cash-for-keys agreements offer a cost-effective alternative to eviction or foreclosure, reducing the time, expenses, and legal fees associated with formal legal proceedings, eviction notices, and property management.

- *Preservation of Property Value:*

Promptly transferring possession of the property through cash for keys agreements helps preserve the property's value by minimizing vacancy periods, enabling timely property maintenance, and facilitating faster resale or rental opportunities.

Loan Repurchase:

In some cases, the original lender may repurchase the nonperforming loan from the investor at a discounted price. This allows the lender to regain control of the loan and pursue alternative resolution strategies such as loan modification or refinancing. Loan repurchase agreements allow lenders to mitigate losses and salvage troubled loans. If you have purchased a partial note from another investor, that investor will want to protect their interest. They may purchase the note back from you or supervise the mitigation process on your behalf if you do not have experience in these matters.

Foreclosure:

Judicial vs. Non-Judicial Foreclosure: Implications for Note Investors

As a note investor, understanding the differences between judicial and non-judicial foreclosure processes is crucial when evaluating the potential acquisition of nonperforming loans (NPLs). Here's how judicial and non-judicial foreclosure states can impact your investment decisions:

Judicial Foreclosure States:

In states that follow a judicial foreclosure process, note investors should be prepared for longer foreclosure timelines and higher legal expenses. Here are some key considerations:

- *Timeline and Costs:*

Judicial foreclosure proceedings typically involve court oversight and legal proceedings, which can prolong the foreclosure process and increase legal expenses for the lender or note investor. As a result, note investors should factor in the additional time and costs associated with judicial foreclosures when assessing the potential return on investment.

- *Legal Requirements:*

Judicial foreclosure states often have stringent legal requirements and procedural rules governing foreclosure proceedings. Note investors must ensure compliance with these requirements to avoid delays or legal challenges that could impact the foreclosure process.

Non-Judicial Foreclosure States:

Non-judicial foreclosure states offer note investors the potential for quicker foreclosure timelines and lower legal expenses. Here's what to consider:

- *Efficiency and Expediency:*

Non-judicial foreclosure proceedings are typically conducted outside of court, allowing for a more streamlined and expedited foreclosure process. Note investors may benefit from shorter timelines and reduced legal costs compared to judicial foreclosures.

- *Trustee Sale Dynamics:*

Trustee sales are commonly used to auction off foreclosed properties in non-judicial foreclosure states. Note investors should familiarize themselves with the trustee sale process, including notice requirements, auction procedures, and redemption rights, to effectively navigate the foreclosure process.

Key Considerations for Note Investors:

- *Risk Assessment:*

When evaluating NPLs in judicial and non-judicial foreclosure states, note investors should assess the inherent risks and challenges associated with each foreclosure process. Consider factors such as foreclosure timelines, legal expenses, borrower rights, and the likelihood of successful resolution.

- *Due Diligence:*

Conduct thorough due diligence on NPLs in both judicial and non-judicial foreclosure states to assess the underlying collateral, borrower financials, and potential obstacles to foreclosure. Evaluate the feasibility of foreclosure strategies and loss mitigation options based on each state's legal and regulatory framework.

- *Working with an Attorney:*

Note investors need to work with an attorney familiar with the foreclosure laws and procedures in the state where the foreclosure is to occur. Some loan servicing companies may have staff attorneys to handle foreclosure proceedings, while others may require investors to retain legal counsel. An experienced attorney can provide valuable guidance and representation throughout the foreclosure process, ensuring compliance with legal requirements and protecting the investor's interests.

Public Auction or Sheriff's Sale: Post Foreclosure Process

Public auctions or sheriff's sales represent the final stage of the foreclosure process, culminating in the sale of the foreclosed property to the highest bidder. State laws and court procedures govern determining the starting bid price, conducting the auction, and distributing proceeds to maximize recovery for creditors while providing fair opportunities for bidders to acquire distressed properties.

Once the foreclosure process is complete and the property is scheduled for public auction or sheriff's sale, several vital steps occur, including the determination of the starting bid price:

Setting the Starting Bid Price:

- *Assessment of Debt Obligations:*

Before the auction, the lender or foreclosing party assesses the total debt obligations associated with the property, including the unpaid loan balance, accrued interest, legal fees, and any additional costs incurred during foreclosure.

- *Evaluation of Property Value:*

The lender or foreclosing party may evaluate the property to determine its current market value. This valuation helps establish an appropriate starting bid price that reflects the property's worth and ensures the lender recovers as much outstanding debt as possible.

- *Consideration of Liens and Encumbrances:*

The starting bid price considers any senior liens, junior liens, or other encumbrances on the property. These liens may include property taxes, homeowners 'association dues, mechanic's liens, or judgments that must be satisfied from the sale proceeds.

- *Legal Requirements:*

State laws and regulations govern determining the starting bid price for public auctions or sheriff's sales. Some states mandate specific formulas or procedures for setting the bid price, while others grant discretion to the foreclosing party or the court overseeing the foreclosure proceedings.

Conducting the Auction:

- *Public Notice:*

The foreclosure auction is publicly advertised to notify interested buyers and potential bidders. Notices are typically published in local newspapers, posted at the courthouse, or advertised through online platforms designated for foreclosure sales.

- *Auction Venue:*

The auction is conducted at a designated time and location, often at the courthouse or another public venue. Sometimes, auctions may be held online, allowing bidders to participate remotely.

- *Bidding Process:*

Interested bidders attend the auction and submit bids for the property. Depending on the auction rules and procedures specified by state law or court order, bidding may start at the predetermined starting bid price or a lower amount.

- *Highest Bidder:*

The property is sold to the highest bidder at or above the starting bid price. The winning bidder is required to provide a deposit or down payment immediately following the auction, with the remaining balance due within a specified timeframe.

- *Distribution of Proceeds:*

Priority of Claims: Proceeds from the sale are distributed according to the priority of claims, with senior lienholders and creditors receiving payment first. Any surplus funds remaining after satisfying the debt obligations are typically returned to the property owner or designated parties, subject to court approval.

Post-Auction Procedures:

- *Confirmation of Sale:*

Following the auction, the sale may be subject to confirmation by the court overseeing the foreclosure proceedings. Confirmation ensures that the sale was conducted correctly and that the highest bid price is fair and reasonable.

- *Issuance of Deed:*

Upon confirmation of the sale, a deed or certificate of sale is issued to the winning bidder, transferring ownership of the property. The new owner assumes responsibility for any remaining obligations or encumbrances on the property.

Unsold Property at Auction: Transition to Real Estate Owned (REO) Status

When a foreclosed property fails to sell at auction, it becomes real estate owned (REO) by the foreclosing lender or institution. Here's what happens after an unsuccessful auction:

Post-Auction Assessment:

- *Evaluation of Bidding Activity:*

If the property does not attract sufficient bids to meet the lender's minimum reserve price or starting bid, it remains unsold at auction. This outcome prompts the lender to reassess the property's value and consider alternative strategies for disposition.

- *Decision Making:*

The lender evaluates the property's condition, marketability, and potential for resale to determine the most appropriate course of action. Property location, market conditions, and prevailing demand influence the decision-making process.

- *Transition to REO Status:*

Transfer of Ownership: Upon unsuccessful auction, property ownership reverts to the foreclosing lender or institution, officially designating it as real estate owned (REO). The lender assumes responsibility for managing the property and addressing any outstanding liens or encumbrances.

REO Property Management:

- *Property Preservation:*

The lender initiates measures to preserve and maintain the REO property, ensuring it remains marketable during the disposition process. This may involve securing the property, performing necessary repairs or renovations, and addressing safety or code compliance issues.

- *Asset Management:*

The lender may engage asset or property management companies to oversee the REO portfolio and coordinate property-related activities, including inspections, maintenance, and marketing.

Marketing and Sales Strategy:

- *Listing the Property:*

The lender collaborates with real estate agents or brokers to list the REO property for sale on the open market. Comprehensive marketing efforts are undertaken to attract potential buyers and expedite the sale process.

- *Price Determination:*

The lender establishes a competitive listing price for the REO property based on market analysis, property condition, and comparable sales in the area. Pricing strategies may vary to optimize market exposure and generate buyer interest.

- *Renovation and Flipping:*

Sometimes, the lender may renovate the REO property to enhance its market appeal and increase its value. Renovation projects may include cosmetic updates, repairs, or major renovations to modernize the property and attract buyers seeking move-in-ready homes.

- *Seller Financing:*

Another strategy is to offer seller financing, where the lender provides financing to the buyer for the purchase of the REO property. This option can expand the pool of potential buyers, particularly those needing help to secure traditional bank financing. The lender becomes the note holder, receiving monthly payments from the buyer and potentially creating a new note investment opportunity.

- *Marketing Campaigns:*

Targeted marketing campaigns, including online listings, open houses, and direct mail campaigns, are implemented to promote the REO property to potential buyers. Effective marketing strategies aim to generate buyer interest and facilitate property sales within a reasonable timeframe.

Sales Transaction:

- *Offer Review:*

The lender evaluates offers submitted by prospective buyers, considering purchase price, terms, and financing contingencies. Multiple offers may be presented, and negotiations may occur to reach a mutually acceptable agreement.

- *Acceptance and Closing:*

Upon acceptance of an offer, the lender proceeds to closing, executes legal documents, and transfers property ownership to the buyer. The sale proceeds offset the outstanding debt and expenses associated with the foreclosure process.

CONCLUSION:

Unsold properties at foreclosure auctions transition to real estate owned (REO) status, marking the beginning of a new phase in the disposition process. While the transition from foreclosure to REO status may initially seem like a setback, savvy investors recognize the opportunity to turn lemons into lemonade through creative disposition strategies.

Investors can capitalize on their REO properties by implementing innovative strategies such as renovation and flipping, offering seller financing, or exploring alternative marketing approaches. By thinking outside the box and leveraging their expertise, investors can maximize the potential of REO properties and generate a solid return on investment.

When an investor acquires an REO property due to investing in nonperforming loans (NPLs) or experiencing a performing note gone bad, strategic planning and creativity can lead to profitable outcomes. Despite the challenges presented by REO properties, investors can find ways to unlock value and achieve a positive ROI, demonstrating the resilience and adaptability of seasoned real estate professionals.

Chapter 12

Wading Into Deeper Notes Water: The Power of Partials

The Power of Partials:

Another option for note investors is to purchase a partial note. This is a good option for investors seeking cash flow and those new to notes who wish to dip their toes in the water. A new investor can invest in a note while finding reassurance that an experienced investor holds the back end of the note and will safeguard their interest.

Moreover, since the experienced investor selling the partial has likely conducted due diligence, a new investor can review it, needing only to update aspects like a title search or broker's price opinion on the property.

As you gain more experience in investing, you could become the investor who acquires the entire note and then sells a partial share of that same note. Picture it like buying or making a whole pizza and then selling a slice to someone else. The difference here is that the other person gets to enjoy their slice first before you can either consume or sell more slices.

It's feasible to buy a note and then sell a fractional interest, sharing the monthly payments with another investor. However, strict regulations govern this fractionalization of notes, necessitating compliance with regulations set forth by the Securities and Exchange Commission. Investors should consult with an attorney to ensure their paperwork complies with these regulations and engage a servicer experienced in servicing fractionalized notes.

For seasoned investors, partials offer a potent method to expand their portfolio. This approach enables investors to purchase a note at a discount with a specific interest rate and then sell a portion to another investor at a slightly lower interest rate. Investors can then reinvest the capital in another note. This strategy allows investors to recover most, if not all, of their investment while retaining ownership of many months of payments on the back end of the note. It's an excellent strategy for retirement accounts such as Roth IRAs. The effectiveness of this partial strategy is illustrated in an upcoming chapter through a real case study.

"Tape" Note Investing:

A "tape" refers to a spreadsheet or list containing detailed information about a portfolio of notes (loans) available for sale. The seller, often a bank or other financial institution, provides this list to potential buyers. The tape is an essential tool for note investors, as it offers a comprehensive overview of the assets, enabling informed investment decisions.

What Does a Tape Include?

A tape typically includes various details about each note, such as:

- Loan Type: Whether the loan is residential or commercial, performing or nonperforming.
- Outstanding Balance: The current unpaid balance on the loan.
- Interest Rate: The rate at which interest is accruing on the loan.
- Maturity Date: When the loan is due to be paid in full.
- Payment History: Information about the borrower's payment history, including any delinquencies or defaults.
- Property Details: Information about the property securing the loan, including its location, type, and current market value.
- Borrower Details: Information about the borrower, including credit score and financial health.

Pros of Purchasing a Tape:

- *Diversification: Spreading Risk Across Multiple Assets*

One of the most compelling advantages of purchasing a tape in note investing is its inherent diversification. Diversification is a risk management strategy involving spreading capital across various assets to reduce exposure to any asset's risk. By acquiring a tape, investors can instantly diversify their portfolio, leading to more stable and predictable returns. Here's a deeper look into how diversification through tape purchasing works and its benefits.

- *Mitigating Individual Note Risk*

When investors purchase a single note, their investment performance is tied directly to the loan's success or failure. If the borrower defaults or the property securing the note declines in value, the investor could face significant losses. However, purchasing a tape that includes multiple notes dilutes the impact of any single note's underperformance across the broader portfolio. This means that the default or poor performance of one note can be offset by the steady performance of others, leading to a more balanced and resilient investment portfolio.

- *Exposure to Different Geographical Markets*

Tapes often include notes secured by properties located in various geographical regions. This geographic diversification is crucial because it spreads exposure to regional economic conditions, property market trends, and local regulatory environments. For instance, an economic downturn in one region might negatively impact property values and borrower performance. Still, notes secured by properties in other, more stable regions may remain unaffected or even thrive. This balance helps to stabilize the overall performance of the investment portfolio.

- Variety in Loan Types and Terms

A tape typically contains different loan types, such as residential, commercial, performing, and nonperforming notes. It may also include loans with varying interest rates, maturity dates, and terms. This variety can provide a steady income stream from performing notes while offering the potential for higher returns from rehabilitating nonperforming loans. Investing in various loan types and terms allows investors to balance their need for immediate cash flow with long-term capital appreciation.

- *Reducing Sector-Specific Risks*

Economic sectors can exhibit varied performance trends based on market cycles, regulatory changes, and economic conditions. For example, residential real estate might perform differently from commercial real estate due to distinct market drivers. By purchasing a tape that includes notes from various sectors, investors reduce their exposure to sector-specific risks. This means that even if one sector faces a downturn, other sectors in the portfolio may continue to perform well, ensuring more stable overall returns.

- *Enhancing Portfolio Liquidity*

A diversified tape can also enhance the liquidity of an investor's portfolio. With a range of notes, there may be opportunities to sell individual notes or smaller subsets of the tape more easily than selling a single large, less liquid asset. This flexibility can be particularly valuable in responding to changing market conditions or meeting liquidity needs without liquidating the entire investment.

- *Leveraging Bulk Purchase Discounts*

When purchasing a tape, investors often have the opportunity to negotiate bulk purchase discounts with the seller. This can result in buying notes at a lower cost per note than buying individually. The cost savings from bulk discounts can improve the overall return on investment and provide a buffer against potential losses.

Cons of Purchasing a Tape:

While purchasing a tape in note investing offers significant advantages, such as diversification and efficiency, it also comes with challenges and potential drawbacks. Understanding these cons is essential for investors to make informed decisions and mitigate risks effectively.

- *Due Diligence Complexity*

Conducting thorough due diligence on an extensive portfolio of notes can be highly complex and time-consuming. Each note within a tape requires individual analysis to assess its risk and potential return. This extensive due diligence process requires significant resources, expertise, and time, potentially leading to increased costs and delays in investment decision-making.

- *Hidden Risks*

A tape may include notes with hidden or hard-to-detect issues that can negatively impact the overall investment. Some of these risks include:

- Problematic Borrowers: Borrowers with financial difficulties or a history of defaults might be challenging to identify without in-depth analysis.
- Property Issues: The properties securing the notes might have undisclosed problems, such as structural damage, environmental hazards, or zoning issues, that affect their value and marketability.
- Fraud and Misrepresentation: There is a risk of fraud or misrepresentation in the information provided by the seller, leading to inaccurate assessments of note quality and value. Sometimes, sellers try to pass off a problematic note hidden within the list of other higher-quality assets. It allows unscrupulous note brokers to unload notes they do not want to deal with.

These hidden risks can result in unexpected losses and reduced returns, making it crucial for investors to employ robust due diligence processes.

Capital Requirements:

Purchasing a tape often requires substantial capital investment, which may only be feasible for some investors. The need for significant upfront capital can limit the ability of smaller investors to participate in such transactions. Additionally, tying up a large amount of capital in a single investment can reduce liquidity and flexibility, potentially impacting the investor's ability to respond to other opportunities or financial needs.

Management Challenges:

Managing an extensive portfolio of notes presents numerous challenges, including:

- Collections and Servicing: Effectively managing payment collection, addressing delinquencies, and handling loan modifications or foreclosures requires efficient servicing operations. Each note will incur a separate servicing fee depending on the level of service needed.
- Legal Actions: Handling legal proceedings related to defaults or disputes can be time-consuming and costly.
- Asset Management: Overseeing and maintaining the properties securing the loans, especially for nonperforming notes, demands substantial effort and resources.

These challenges necessitate robust systems, processes, and experienced personnel to manage the portfolio effectively.

Market Volatility:

Market volatility and economic changes can significantly affect the value of the notes within a tape. Factors such as interest rate fluctuations, changes in property values, and economic downturns can impact the notes' performance. For instance:

- Interest Rate Risk: Rising interest rates can increase defaults on adjustable-rate mortgages or reduce the value of fixed-rate notes.
- Property Market Conditions: Declining property values can result in higher loan-to-value (LTV) ratios, increasing the risk of borrower defaults and reducing the recoverable amount in case of foreclosure.
- Economic Shifts: Economic downturns or regional economic issues can affect borrowers' ability to make payments, leading to higher default rates.

These factors can lead to unpredictable returns and potential losses, underscoring the importance of market analysis and risk management strategies.

Hypothecation: A Strategy for Truly Passive Returns

Hypothecation is a financial term relevant to note investing. It is a mechanism for passive investors to achieve a stable rate of return while enjoying the security of having their loan backed by the note's value.

In essence, hypothecation involves pledging a note or a group of notes as collateral for a loan. This strategy presents an attractive opportunity for passive investors seeking a more hands-off approach to note investing. Here's how it typically works:

- *Collateralized Investment:*

By entering into a hypothecation agreement, the passive investor essentially lends money to a note investor (typically a business), who pledges one or more notes as collateral for the loan. This means that if the borrower defaults on the loan, the passive investor has a claim to the collateralized notes, providing security for their investment.

- *Stable Rate of Return:*

In return for providing the loan, the passive investor receives a specified interest rate of return, paid monthly, quarterly, or annually. This predictable income stream offers a stable rate of return, making hypothecation an appealing option for investors seeking consistent cash flow without actively managing their investments.

- *Security of Investment:*

Unlike some other forms of investing where the returns are subject to market fluctuations or the performance of specific assets, hypothecation offers a level of security tied directly to the value of the underlying notes. Since the notes themselves collateralize the loan, the passive investor can have confidence in the stability of their investment, even in uncertain market conditions.

- *Flexibility in Income:*

Depending on the terms of the hypothecation agreement, passive investors may have the flexibility to reinvest their interest payments with the experienced investor, compounding their returns over time.

142

Alternatively, they may receive the interest payments as cash income, providing a steady source of passive income.

- *Tax Considerations:*

Passive investors need to consult with their tax professionals regarding the tax implications of hypothecation. Depending on the structure of the agreement and the jurisdiction, interest income from hypothecated notes may be subject to taxation.

The note investor should also provide the passive investor with a 1099-INT for tax reporting purposes.

When executed by lending to an expert investor with a diversified note portfolio, hypothecation is a robust strategy for mitigating risk in note investing. Let's delve into how this approach enhances risk management:

Expertise and Experience:

Expert note investors typically possess extensive experience and expertise in analyzing, acquiring, and managing notes. Passive investors benefit from these professionals' seasoned judgment and skill set by lending to such individuals. Expert investors are adept at identifying high-quality notes and navigating potential pitfalls, thereby reducing the overall risk associated with the investment.

- *Diversification:*

Diversification is a cornerstone of effective risk management in investment portfolios. Expert note investors often maintain diversified portfolios comprising notes across various asset classes, geographical locations, and risk profiles. By lending to these investors, passive investors indirectly gain exposure to a broad spectrum of notes, spreading risk across different properties and borrowers. This diversification helps mitigate the impact of any adverse developments affecting individual notes or sectors. In some cases, however, investors may only pledge a single note for hypothecation.

- *Collateralized Security:*

In a hypothecation arrangement, the loan extended by the passive investor is secured by the collateral of a single note or a note portfolio held by the expert investor. The diversified nature of this portfolio provides additional security, as the value of the collateral is spread across multiple assets. In the event of default by the borrower, the passive investor can rely on the diversified portfolio to recoup their investment.

- *Risk-Adjusted Returns:*

Passive investors can achieve attractive risk-adjusted returns by lending to an expert investor with a diversified note portfolio. The expertise and diversification employed by the expert investor help optimize the risk-return profile of the investment, aiming to maximize returns while minimizing downside risk. This alignment of risk and reward is crucial for passive investors seeking stable income generation with prudent risk management.

- *Monitoring and Oversight:*

Expert investors typically maintain rigorous monitoring and oversight mechanisms to track the performance of their note portfolio and ensure compliance with loan agreements. Passive investors benefit from this diligent supervision, as it helps detect and address potential issues proactively, further enhancing risk mitigation efforts.

CONCLUSION:

Hypothecation to expert investors with diversified note portfolios offers a compelling avenue for passive investors to mitigate risk in note investing. Leveraging the expertise, diversification, collateralized security, and diligent oversight these seasoned professionals provide, passive investors can pursue attractive risk-adjusted returns while minimizing exposure to adverse market conditions and individual note defaults.

In summary, hypothecation offers passive investors an opportunity to participate in note investing while enjoying the benefits of a stable rate of return and the security of having their investment collateralized by the value of the underlying notes. By partnering with experienced note investors and understanding the terms of the hypothecation agreement, passive investors can effectively leverage this strategy to grow their wealth with confidence.

CHAPTER 13

Note Investing: Putting It All Together

Maximizing Your Returns:

Asset Management: Maximizing Returns

Effective asset management is paramount to maximizing returns and preserving the value of investments. By employing proactive strategies and staying abreast of market dynamics and regulatory developments, investors can optimize the performance of their note portfolios. Let's delve into the key components of effective asset management in note investing:

- *Proactive Communication with Loan Servicers:*

Maintaining open and proactive communication with loan servicing companies is essential for ensuring the smooth operation of note investments. Investors should regularly engage with servicers to monitor payment performance, address borrower inquiries or concerns, and promptly resolve any issues that may arise. By fostering a collaborative relationship with servicers, investors can ensure timely payment processing, mitigate potential delinquencies, and safeguard the integrity of their investments.

- *Restructuring Distressed Loans:*

When faced with distressed loans or borrowers experiencing financial hardships, proactive loan restructuring can mitigate losses and preserve asset value. Investors should assess the borrower's financial situation, explore alternative payment arrangements, and consider loan modifications or workout plans tailored to the borrower's circumstances. By offering flexible solutions and support to distressed borrowers, investors can increase the likelihood of loan rehabilitation and minimize default risk.

- *Initiating Foreclosure Proceedings:*

In cases where loan default becomes inevitable and all efforts to restructure the loan have been exhausted, initiating foreclosure proceedings may be necessary to protect investors' interests. Investors should work closely with legal counsel and loan servicing companies to navigate the foreclosure process efficiently and comply with applicable laws and regulations. By taking timely and decisive action to address default situations, investors can minimize losses and maximize recovery on nonperforming assets.

Market Trends and Regulatory Changes:

Staying informed about market trends, economic indicators, and regulatory changes is essential for adapting investment strategies and mitigating risks in note investing.

Investors should closely monitor interest rate movements, property market dynamics, and legislative developments impacting the mortgage industry. By staying ahead of the curve and adjusting investment strategies accordingly, investors can capitalize on emerging opportunities, mitigate potential threats, and preserve the long-term value of their note portfolios.

Exit Strategies: Knowing When to Hold and When to Fold

Developing a clear exit strategy is crucial for real estate note investors. Whether the goal is to collect interest payments over the life of the note, sell the note for a profit, or foreclose on the property, having a well-defined plan can significantly impact the investment's success. Flexibility to adjust strategies in response to market conditions and investment performance can further enhance returns, enabling investors to capitalize on opportunities and mitigate losses.

Importance of Asset Protection:

Asset protection is critical to any investment strategy, especially in real estate, where potential liabilities can be significant. Let's delve into the importance of investing within an LLC, a trust, or another asset protection structure and explore some key considerations:

- *Limiting Personal Liability:*

Investing in real estate inherently carries risks, including the possibility of lawsuits arising from tenant disputes, property damage, or other unforeseen circumstances. By holding real estate assets within a protective structure, such as an LLC or trust, investors can shield their assets from potential litigation and limit their liability exposure.

- *Preserving Wealth:*

Asset protection structures help safeguard the wealth accumulated through real estate investments. In the event of a lawsuit or creditor claim, protected assets are less vulnerable to seizure, allowing investors to preserve their hard-earned wealth and financial security.

- *Enhancing Privacy:*

Certain asset protection vehicles like trusts offer enhanced privacy by keeping ownership details confidential. This can benefit investors who prefer anonymity and protect their privacy from public scrutiny.

- *Facilitating Estate Planning:*

Asset protection structures can also serve estate planning purposes by allowing investors to transfer real estate assets to future generations while minimizing tax liabilities and preserving family wealth for heirs and beneficiaries.

Investing within an LLC:

- *Limited Liability Protection:*

Limited liability companies (LLCs) are popular among real estate investors due to their flexible structure and strong liability protection. By holding real estate assets within an LLC, investors shield their assets from claims arising from the property's operations or ownership.

- *Pass-Through Taxation:*

LLCs offer pass-through taxation, meaning that profits and losses from the real estate investments flow through to the individual members' tax returns. This can result in tax advantages and simplify tax reporting for investors.

- *Separation of Assets:*

Establishing separate LLCs for each real estate property or portfolio of properties allows investors to compartmentalize their assets and liabilities. This ensures that liabilities associated with one property do not jeopardize the assets held in other LLCs.

- *Professional Management:*

Structuring real estate investments within an LLC can facilitate professional management by allowing investors to bring in partners or hire property managers while maintaining control and protecting their assets.

Investing within a Trust:

- *Asset Protection:*

Trusts offer asset protection by holding real estate assets on behalf of beneficiaries, thereby separating ownership from direct control. Investors can retain varying degrees of control and protection depending on the type of trust used, such as a revocable living or an irrevocable trust.

- *Estate Planning Benefits:*

Trusts are valuable tools for estate planning. They allow investors to transfer real estate assets to heirs and beneficiaries while avoiding probate and minimizing estate taxes. Trusts can also provide for the management and distribution of assets according to the investor's wishes.

- *Privacy:*

Trusts offer enhanced privacy by keeping ownership details confidential. This can be particularly beneficial for high-profile investors or those seeking to shield their real estate holdings from public scrutiny.

- *Flexibility:*

Trusts offer flexibility in structuring ownership and management arrangements for real estate assets. Investors can designate trustees to manage the trust property, establish specific distribution instructions, and customize the trust terms to meet their unique needs and objectives.

Other Asset Protection Structures:

In addition to LLCs and trusts, investors may consider other asset protection structures, such as limited partnerships (LPs), limited liability partnerships (LLPs), or asset protection trusts (APTs), depending on their specific goals, jurisdictional considerations, and risk tolerance.

- *Asset Protection Strategies within Self-Directed IRAs for Real Estate Note Investing: Diversification of Note Investments:*

Diversifying investments within a self-directed IRA focused on real estate notes can help spread risk across various types of notes, borrowers, and geographic locations. By diversifying, investors can reduce exposure to any single borrower default or market downturn.

- *Limited Liability Entities:*

Holding real estate notes within limited liability entities like LLCs can provide additional protection against potential liabilities. Investors can set up an LLC owned by the self-directed IRA to hold the notes, shielding their assets from litigation or claims related to the notes.

- *Insurance Coverage:*

Investors may consider obtaining insurance coverage to mitigate specific risks depending on the type of real estate notes held within the IRA. For example, investors holding mortgage notes secured by properties may explore title or mortgage insurance to protect against title defects or borrower default.

- *Asset Protection Trusts:*

In permitted jurisdictions, investors may establish asset protection trusts (APTs) within their self-directed IRAs to safeguard real estate note investments from creditors and legal judgments. APTs can offer additional protection while allowing investors to benefit from tax-deferred growth.

- *Custodial Protection:*

Working with a reputable IRA custodian specializing in self-directed IRAs for real estate note investing is essential. A qualified custodian can ensure compliance with IRS regulations, safeguard assets, and provide expert guidance on asset protection strategies tailored to real estate note investments.

Scenario 1: "Sarah's" Example of Asset Protection within a Self-Directed IRA for Real Estate Note Investing:

Sarah wants to diversify her retirement portfolio as a real estate note investor by investing in various mortgage notes within her self-directed IRA. She's concerned about protecting her retirement savings from potential liabilities associated with note investments.

- *Asset Protection Strategy:*

To protect her real estate note investments within the self-directed IRA, Sarah implements the following strategies:

- *Establishment of an LLC:*

Sarah forms a single-member LLC (SMLLC) owned by her self-directed IRA and directs the IRA custodian to purchase membership interests using funds from the IRA.

- *Ownership of Mortgage Notes:*

The SMLLC, acting as the investment vehicle for the IRA, purchases mortgage notes under its name. The ownership of each note is held in the name of the LLC, providing limited liability protection for Sarah's assets.

- *Risk Mitigation:*

Sarah conducts thorough due diligence on each mortgage note investment, assessing borrower creditworthiness, property value, and loan-to-value ratios. She also ensures that appropriate loan documentation, including promissory notes and deeds of trust, are in place to protect her interests.

- *Insurance Considerations:*

Sarah explores insurance options, such as errors and omissions (E&O) insurance or fidelity bond coverage, to protect against potential losses arising from errors in loan servicing or fraudulent activities by borrowers.

- *Regular Monitoring and Review:*

Sarah regularly oversees her real estate note investments within the self-directed IRA, monitoring payment performance, assessing market conditions, and adjusting her investment strategy to mitigate risks and maximize returns.

Scenario 2: Asset Protection and Self-Directed Individual Retirement Accounts (SDIRA) Hypothecation Strategy for Real Estate Note Investing within Self-Directed IRAs:

- *Hypothecation Overview:*

In this scenario, the IRA account holder lends funds from their self-directed IRA to a professional investor who specializes in managing real estate notes. The experienced investor holds and manages all aspects of the real estate notes, while the IRA account holder receives a fixed rate of return on their investment. The real estate notes held by the professional investor serve as collateral for the loan provided by the IRA account holder, insulating the IRA account holder from direct involvement with the borrower on the notes.

Benefits of Hypothecation:

- *Passive Investment:*

The IRA account holder can invest in real estate notes without actively managing them. By lending funds to a professional investor who manages the notes, the IRA account holder can generate a fixed rate of return without ownership or management responsibilities.

- *Risk Mitigation:*

The IRA account holder is insulated from the borrower on the real estate notes held by the professional investor. Since the IRA account holder does not own or manage the notes directly, they are protected from potential risks associated with borrower default or other liabilities.

- *Anonymity and Confidentiality:*

The professional investor manages the real estate notes on behalf of the IRA account holder, maintaining the account holder's anonymity and privacy. The borrower on the notes is unaware of the IRA account holder's involvement, preserving confidentiality.

- *Simplified Asset Protection:*

Unlike direct ownership of real estate assets, the IRA account holder may not need to create additional legal structures, such as LLCs or trusts, to protect their investment. The hypothecation strategy allows passive investment within the self-directed IRA while benefiting from asset protection.

- *Consultation with an Experienced IRA Account Manager:*

Given the complexity of self-directed IRAs and the importance of proper investment strategy execution, IRA account holders must consult with experienced IRA account managers. An experienced IRA account manager can provide personalized guidance and recommendations tailored to the investor's situation, including implementing the hypothecation strategy for real estate note investing.

Scenario 3: Example of Hypothecation Strategy:

Let's illustrate how an IRA account holder could utilize hypothecation to invest in real estate notes within their self-directed IRA passively:

Sarah, an IRA account holder, wants to diversify her retirement portfolio by investing in real estate notes but prefers a passive investment approach.

- *Hypothecation Strategy:*

Sarah identifies an experienced real estate note investor, John, who specializes in acquiring and managing notes. John offers Sarah a fixed rate of return in exchange for lending funds from her self-directed IRA.

- *Loan Agreement:*

Sarah and John enter a loan agreement in which Sarah's self-directed IRA lends funds to John. The funds provided are a loan, with John's real estate notes as collateral.

- *Fixed Rate of Return:*

John agrees to pay Sarah a fixed rate of return on the loan provided by her self-directed IRA. The rate of return is predetermined and agreed upon in the loan agreement.

- *Passive Investment:*

Sarah's self-directed IRA receives a fixed rate of return without needing active involvement in managing the real estate notes. John handles all aspects of acquiring, managing, and servicing the notes on behalf of Sarah's IRA.

- *Risk Mitigation:*

Since the real estate notes serve as collateral for the loan provided by Sarah's IRA, she is insulated from direct exposure to the borrower on the notes. As a professional investor, John bears any potential risks associated with borrower default or other liabilities.

When to Cash Out:

In the realm of real estate note investing, timing is everything. This investment strategy, involving the purchase of the debt secured by a property rather than the property itself, offers a unique blend of opportunities and challenges. Understanding when to sell or exit such an investment is crucial for maximizing gains or minimizing losses. Unfortunately, many investors struggle to recognize the optimal moment to move, leading to missed opportunities or exacerbated financial setbacks.

The primary challenge in real estate note investing lies in accurately predicting the market's direction and assessing the borrower's ability to continue making payments. The scale of this issue is significant, as premature exits can result in lost profits, while delayed actions might lead to unrecoverable losses. The implications are far-reaching, affecting individual investors and the broader financial ecosystem, as poorly timed decisions can contribute to market instability.

If this problem remains unresolved, investors risk facing adverse outcomes such as diminished returns, capital erosion, and, in worst-case scenarios, total investment loss. Historical data shows that investors who fail to act at the right time can see their expected returns halve, if not more. For instance, a delay in selling or exiting an underperforming note can lead to a situation where the recoverable value diminishes due to deteriorating property conditions or further declines in the borrower's financial stability.

To overcome this challenge, it is crucial to develop a comprehensive exit strategy based on a thorough market analysis and a clear understanding of one's investment objectives. This approach requires investors to stay informed about market trends, regulatory changes, and the borrower's financial health, using these insights to make timely decisions.

Implementing this solution involves several key steps. Firstly, investors must establish clear criteria for selling or exiting, such as reaching a specific return threshold or identifying signs of market downturns. Regularly reviewing the investment's performance against these criteria is essential. Secondly, staying abreast of market developments enables investors to anticipate changes that might affect their investment. Thirdly, effective communication with the borrower can provide early warnings of potential payment issues. Potential challenges in this approach include information overload and analysis paralysis. However, these can be mitigated through a disciplined focus on relevant data and consultation with financial advisors.

Past outcomes demonstrate the effectiveness of this strategy. Investors who have applied a disciplined approach to their exit strategy consistently outperformed those who act impulsively or hold onto their investments for too long. For example, a study of real estate note sales over the past decade revealed that timely exits based on strategic criteria yielded an average of 20% higher returns than delayed decisions.

Other solutions (like refinancing or restructuring the note) may offer alternative ways to address underperformance. However, they often involve additional complexities and uncertainties. These approaches can sometimes salvage an investment, but they typically provide a different return maximization or loss minimization level than a well-timed exit strategy.

Early Payout: Plan For It!

Let's discuss what happens when a note pays out before maturity, including reasons for early payout and how investors prepare for this scenario:

- *Refinancing:*

Borrowers may refinance their loans to take advantage of lower interest rates, reduce monthly payments, or access equity in the property. Refinancing often results in the early repayment of the existing note.

- *Sale of Property:*

If the property securing the note sells, the proceeds from the sale are used to repay the outstanding loan balance, resulting in an early payout of the note.

- *Prepayment:*

Some loan agreements allow borrowers to make prepayments on their loans, in part or whole, without penalty. Borrowers may make prepayments to reduce interest costs or shorten the loan term, leading to an early payoff of the note.

- *Default:*

In some cases, borrowers may default on their loans, leading to foreclosure or other remedies that result in the early liquidation of the note.

Being Prepared for Early Payout:

- *Monitor Loan Performance:*

Monitor the performance of the notes in your portfolio regularly to identify any signs of potential early payoff. Stay informed about market conditions, borrower behavior, and other factors impacting loan repayment.

- *Diversification:*

Maintain a diversified portfolio of notes to spread risk across different borrowers, loan types, and geographic locations. Diversification can mitigate the impact of early payouts on your overall investment returns.

- *Reinvestment Strategy:*

Develop a reinvestment strategy to redeploy funds from early payout events. When determining how to reinvest the proceeds from matured or prepaid notes, consider your investment goals, risk tolerance, and market conditions.

- *Liquidity Management:*

Ensure you have sufficient liquidity in your investment accounts to handle early payout events and take advantage of new investment opportunities. Having readily available funds allows you to react quickly to market changes and deploy capital effectively.

- *Stay Proactive:*

Stay proactive in managing your note portfolio, and be prepared to act swiftly when early payout events occur. Evaluate the potential impact on your investment strategy and adjust your approach accordingly to maintain portfolio performance.

Average Note Duration:

Notes pay out on average at around the 8.5-year mark. Investors should be prepared to redeploy funds from prepaid notes approximately every 8.5 years to maintain a consistent investment strategy and maximize returns.

Note early payout is expected in real estate note investing, and investors must be prepared to manage these events effectively. By understanding the reasons for early payout, developing a reinvestment strategy, and staying proactive in portfolio management, investors can navigate early payout events and optimize their investment returns over time. Additionally, being aware of the average note duration can help investors plan for the redeployment of funds and maintain a well-balanced portfolio.

CONCLUSION:

The Power of Compounding:

Real estate notes have emerged as a potent vehicle for generating passive income, offering security and lucrative returns. The essence of this discussion hinges on a systematic, evidence-based analysis of how reinvesting earnings from real estate notes can significantly amplify your retirement savings over time. The importance of an evidence-based approach cannot be overstated; it ensures that our strategies are not based on mere conjecture but are backed by tangible data and proven outcomes.

The core proposition that we aim to scrutinize is the assertion that the strategic reinvestment of earnings from real estate notes into additional notes can compound wealth in a way that far exceeds traditional retirement saving methods. This proposition is not just a theoretical assertion. Still, it is supported by a foundational piece of evidence: a comprehensive study conducted by the National Association of Real Estate Investors (NAREI) in 2020. This study surveyed over 2,000 investors over 15 years, tracking the performance of portfolios that solely relied on the initial investment in real estate notes versus those that consistently reinvested their earnings.

Digging deeper into the study reveals that the methodology was rigorous and expansive. The NAREI ensured a diversified sample by including investors from various geographic locations, investment sizes, and experience levels. This approach bolstered the credibility of the findings by minimizing biases and reflecting a broad spectrum of real estate investment scenarios. The key finding was unequivocal: portfolios that engaged in reinvestment exhibited an average growth rate of 70% higher than those that did not. This stark contrast underscores the profound impact of reinvestment strategies on wealth accumulation over time.

While the evidence strongly supports the initial claim, it is essential to consider potential counterarguments. Critics might point out that reinvesting earnings from real estate notes inherently carries more risk, especially in volatile markets or during economic downturns. This perspective holds merit and emphasizes the importance of a balanced and cautious approach to reinvestment.

It is crucial to highlight the importance of diversification and risk assessment in reinvestment. Further evidence supporting the initial claim can be found in historical market analysis, which shows that well-diversified real estate investment portfolios have consistently outperformed single-asset investments over long periods, even when accounting for economic fluctuations. This reinforces the argument that while reinvestment carries risk, strategic planning and diversification can mitigate these risks effectively.

Further strengthening the claim, another study by the Real Estate Investment Association (REIA) in 2019 highlighted the psychological benefits of reinvestment strategies. It noted that investors who reinvest their earnings tend to be more engaged and proactive in managing their portfolios, leading to better decision-making and higher overall returns.

Applying these evidence-based findings to real-life scenarios reveals that the disciplined reinvestment of earnings from real estate notes can transform a modest initial investment into a substantial retirement nest egg. This strategy not only maximizes the potential for wealth accumulation but also instills a proactive investment mindset critical for long-term financial success.

The broader significance of these findings lies in their ability to offer a viable path to financial independence and security for retirees, challenging conventional retirement planning paradigms and opening up new avenues for wealth generation.

Each investor can decide what strategy is best for their particular situation. An investor can use their portfolio for long-term wealth accumulation, retirement planning, or to use as cash flow today. The beauty of investing in real estate notes is that an investor can combine all three: Plan for retirement, accumulate generational wealth, and supplement their monthly income as needed today. Note investors must remember that monthly payments realized from notes are amortized loans being repaid. This means that a portion of the payment is for interest, and a portion of the payment reduces the principal amount owed. Investors need to track the amortization over time to decide on reinvestment of the repaid principal amount.

CHAPTER 14

Case Studies

The following three case studies were featured at the annual note contest I entered, and they won first place in their category. These are good examples of how investors can make a solid investment from notes and how to respond when things do not go as planned.

Case #1: Tennessee in 2020 Note Expo Award-Winning Deal

I purchased the note on a property in Tennessee on a Land Contract or Agreement for Deed. The time between when I purchased the original note from the private equity fund and sold the partial note was 18 months. As discussed earlier in the book, seeing a deeply discounted note indicates problems. I have found that land contracts are often discounted because they have unique issues, such as the lender being responsible for unpaid taxes or code violations. Although taxes were current and there were no violations on file for this property and there were no violations on file, it is still a responsibility many note investors do not want. In addition, the loan-to-value ratio for this property was 88%, which does not give the lender much room to recover their money if the loan goes bad and the property is sold. Since I purchased this note at a significant discount, the loan-to-value was closer to 75%. Looking at the rest of the neighborhood, I saw the potential to significantly increase the property's value by doing a larger-than-normal renovation.

After purchasing the note, I collected three months of payments with no problem. After those first three payments, the borrower stopped paying. She communicated with the servicing company that she was having significant family problems and financial difficulties. She asked if there was a way to do a forbearance or a loan modification. I asked the servicing company if they could get more details from her on her

161

financial situation. The borrower told them her husband had left and filed for divorce, leaving her without income to contribute to the monthly payment. Her teenage daughter was also having emotional problems and had attempted suicide the previous month. Doing a loan modification would require negotiation with the borrower to get her payment within her budget. The servicing company I used allowed me to contact the borrower directly to negotiate the loan modification terms.

The borrower and I had a difficult discussion about her situation, and we went over her budget in detail to keep her in the house if possible. I had room to lower the unpaid balance amount because I had purchased this note at a significant discount (this is not something I shared with the borrower). We determined what she wanted her monthly payment, which was manageable and realistic. Once that was determined, I adjusted the terms of the note to match this payment. I lowered the unpaid balance amount, reduced the interest rate, and set the remaining term at 300 months- up from 250 months.

Once this was determined, I used an attorney to draw up the new Land Contract. The Land Contracts laws in Tennessee allow the borrower to become a tenant if they are more than 30 days late on a payment. Once they are a tenant, they can be evicted. This process is much less expensive and less time-consuming than a foreclosure process that would be necessary for a note and mortgage where the deed is held in trust. This was a good decision because the borrower defaulted after six payments again, and he disconnected her telephone. She also failed to respond to certified mail. After 30 days, the attorney sent her an eviction notice, and she vacated the property 30 days later. Since this was a land contract, the deed to the property was already in the name of my LLC. Nothing more needed to be done in that respect.

When the borrower vacated the property, she called the servicing company. She notified them that some unknown persons had stolen the plumbing fixtures, the countertops, several cabinets, and the wood from the outside deck. I sent a property preservation company to secure and winterize the property while determining what would be done next. The preservation company found the front door wide open and a large pile of trash in the front yard. In addition to securing and winterizing the property, I had them remove the trash for a small extra fee.

My first thought was to sell this to a real estate wholesaler for just enough to get my money back and move on. However, I looked online at various properties in this neighborhood and determined that if I could find somebody to do a complete renovation, I could do quite well by flipping the house. This property was in a small rural community, and I had difficulty finding contractors who would call me back. The one contractor who called me back said he would look at the property and give me an estimate for a complete renovation. He never called me back and would not return my calls! The property preservation company had sent me photos of the interior and exterior, so I think this contractor was intimidated by how much work was needed.

I had previously met and worked with a contractor in New Jersey who did a complete renovation on a property I had obtained via a nonperforming note I had purchased. I reached out to her to see if I could find a referral for this area in Tennessee. She has several renovation teams working for her, and she said many of her workers would love to go on an adventure out of town. She said if I paid for the fuel, she would send a team there to renovate the house for me. She flew there, rented a car, and drove for almost 3 hours to get to the house to give me a complete estimate. She told me she could convert this from a two-bedroom one-bathroom house, to a three-bedroom two-bath house. It would be a significant renovation, including a new roof, but it could be done. Since she specializes in flipping houses, she also looked around the neighborhood, and we determined that the property could be listed for $190,000. I authorized her to proceed based on her renovation estimate and the potential sale price.

The renovation took about 60 days to complete. A real estate agent went by the property when it was about 50% complete and told the foreman she had a potential buyer. She was given my contact information, and we negotiated a price of $185,000. Her buyers had pre-qualified for a loan, so we entered a sale agreement. We had to wait for the renovation to be complete, so this was a longer-than-average escrow period. During escrow, interest rates were climbing rapidly, and at a certain point, her buyers no longer qualified for the loan. I told her I offer private financing for deserving buyers with a large down payment. This house was perfect for her buyers, so they jumped at the chance to take advantage of my private financing offer.

We agreed on a 15% down payment, and I had the buyers qualified through an RMLO. I did this deal with a conventional note and mortgage because these were solid borrowers compared to those in there before.

I have a pool of investors who invest with me via hypothecation. One of these investors has been very interested in getting more active in note investing and was interested in owning a note himself. Until now, he has been loaning my company money collateralized by notes and getting a good rate of return. I had discussed with him that purchasing partial notes is a way to get his feet wet in direct note investing while having me as a safety net. He would own a partial note, and because I would still own the back end of the note, I would stay on top of things to protect my interest. I gave him copies of all of the collateral documents so he could do his due diligence, and I assisted with this, advising him on what to look for. Although this note did not have much pay history, only three months, he was excited to get more involved by purchasing a partial. He bought 194 months of this note for $125,000, which gave him a good 8.01% return rate.

In summary, I purchased a note on a Land Contract for a property in Tennessee. The borrower defaulted, and I ended up owning a dilapidated house. I flipped the house and sold it with seller financing, making a substantial profit. And I never set foot in Tennessee.

Case #1 Details:

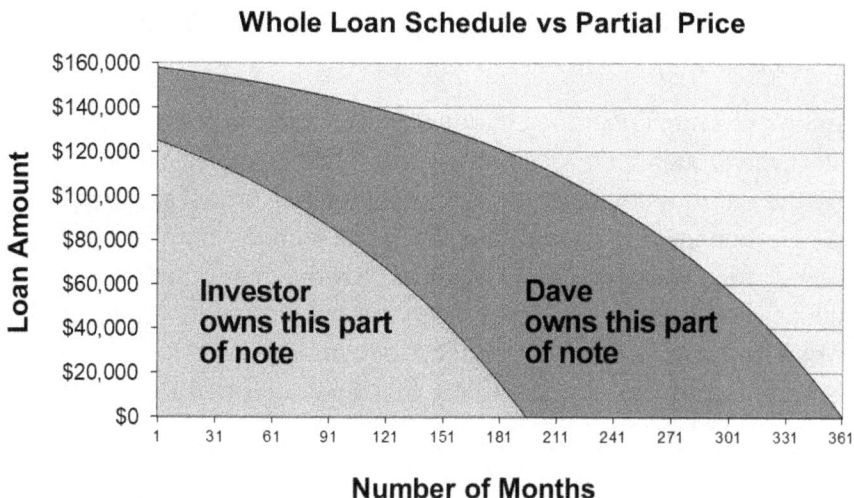

Whole Loan Schedule vs Partial Price

(Chart: Loan Amount vs Number of Months)

- Y-axis (Loan Amount): $0, $20,000, $40,000, $60,000, $80,000, $100,000, $120,000, $140,000, $160,000
- X-axis (Number of Months): 1, 31, 61, 91, 121, 151, 181, 211, 241, 271, 301, 331, 361

Investor owns this part of note

Dave owns this part of note

Number of Months

Case Study #2: New Jersey Note Expo Award-Winning Deal

In June of 2018, I purchased a nonperforming note from a private equity fund. The unpaid balance was $68,638, and I bought the note for $46,310. This was a 33% discount from the note value because of its nonperforming status. The borrower had not made a payment in over a year. During the due diligence process, I discovered that the borrower had died, his family had inherited the house, and it was most of the way through the foreclosure process. This note had been listed for sale by the private equity fund several months previously; however, since the property was in New Jersey, many investors were scared off because it is a judicial foreclosure state. Judicial foreclosures can be more cumbersome, complicated, and expensive.

I did as much due diligence as I could before purchasing the note, and I found that the foreclosure process had been started in August 2017. Since the foreclosure process in New Jersey typically takes about 12 months, I surmised that this foreclosure process was almost complete. After purchasing the note, I contacted the attorney's office and discovered that the foreclosure had been stalled because the family was arguing over who should inherit the house. I had the attorney notify the family that whoever inherited the house would also be responsible for the unpaid balance of the note. A few days later, the attorney informed me that nobody in the family wanted this liability, so there would be nobody to contest the foreclosure.

During this time, I paid the delinquent taxes and the outstanding utility bills. Even though there was nobody to contest the foreclosure, it would take the attorney several months to complete the process. The property was auctioned in December of 2018, and nobody purchased it. The auction price was the unpaid balance plus the cost of the back taxes, utilities, and legal fees. Even though the private equity fund that had owned this note had spent almost $7000 on legal fees for this asset, I was entitled to be reimbursed for that amount since I was now the owner of the note.

I received the deed to the property and explored each exit strategy I had in mind when I initially purchased the note. The easiest and quickest way to exit was with a wholesaler or flipper; however, after talking to several wholesalers and flippers, I was not willing to accept the meager price they were offering. My other exit strategy was to turn this into a turnkey rental property for an investor who likes rentals. With this in mind, I contacted several renovation companies in the area. I hired a small renovation company to complete the property renovation, which was completed in March 2019. My total investment for renovating the house, legal fees, and back taxes was $60,726.

I then retained a property management company that almost immediately found a renter to move in. I sold the property in September of 2019 as a turnkey rental investment to another investor I knew who was looking for a single-family investment property. The sale price was $149,000. Since I had used other investor money (money I had borrowed from others to do this deal), I needed to include this in my calculation to determine my total profit.

The Numbers:

- Note price: $46,310
- Renovation, taxes, utilities: $60,726
- Debt service: $9,314

- TOTAL: $116,360
- Sold for $149,000
- Profit: $32,640 over 15 months – 28.05% ROI (Annualized 21.78%)

But wait, there's more! The septic system backed up a few months after I sold it to the other investor. He called me to get a referral to the septic company that had serviced this system during the renovation. The septic company pumped the tank out several times over the next few months, which is unusual. After a complete inspection of the system, they determined that it was so old and damaged that it needed to be completely replaced. The problem was that it was impossible to completely replace the system and be within the city code, which had been changed several times since the original system was installed. This was quite the dilemma!

There is no city sewer system on this street to which the property could be connected. However, a multifamily building behind this property was connected to the city sewer system. I contacted the owner of this building, who said he would permit an easement allowing us to connect to the sewer system. The only stipulation was that his attorney had to be used.

Connecting to the city sewer system via the multifamily property cost $16,498, and the building owner's attorney charged $7500 to create the easement document. Thus, the total cost for resolving this problem was $23,998.

Legally, I was not responsible for any of this cost because I had sold the property to another investor. Ethically, I felt I was obligated to the other investor because it did not seem right to stick him with the cost of something that probably should have been discovered before the sale. I paid the attorney and the plumbing company to complete this project.

The New Numbers:

- Note price: $46,310
- Renovation, taxes, utilities: $60,726
- Debt service: $9,314

- Plumbing / Septic / Easement cost: $23,998
- TOTAL: $140,358
- Profit: $8,642 - 6.6% ROI (4.88%) annualized.

This is a minimal return for such a large amount of work on a nonperforming loan. This is unusual, but this unforeseen septic system problem threw a giant wrench into my profit. Again, I had no legal obligation to pay for those repairs and legal fees because I had already sold the property. But I always try to do the right thing for the right reason, so I felt I needed to pay for these repairs. Because I treated this investor who purchased the house fairly, he has invested over $500,000 with me since this deal. Also, the mom-and-pop renovation company I used to renovate this property and do some of the repairs after the septic issue was resolved has been doing business with me since then, leading to over $1.2 million in notes as of this writing. My ROI on this deal was big in other ways!

Case Study #3: Pennsylvania

In 2014, a couple purchased a home in Pittsburgh, PA, on an Agreement for Deed, or Land Contract, for $44,000. They made a down payment of $1,460 and took out a loan for $42,540 at 9.9% interest for 360 months. The payment would be $370.18.

An investor new to notes purchased this note on October 16, 2018, for $36,430. The unpaid balance at that time was $41,634.88, as the homeowners had missed payments. Since the investor purchased the note, it has been a sub-performing note, with the borrowers occasionally missing payments and always behind.

In November 2022, the investor received information from the Pennsylvania Attorney General's Office regarding a lawsuit they filed against the note originator in 2018, several months before the investor purchased it. The originator sold approximately one hundred homes using tactics that the Attorney General believed were illegal or did not provide homebuyers with true information. In addition, the interest rate charged on the loan was illegal under the state's usury law. No loan under $50,000 in Pennsylvania can charge an interest rate of more than 6%. A table is updated every month that shows the maximum amount that can be charged, usually less than 6%. They determined the note the investor purchased could be a maximum of 5.5% interest, not 9.9%.

The Attorney General's Office asked that the investor change the agreement with the homebuyers from the Agreement for Deed to a note and mortgage because they believed it gave the homeowners more protection. They also required that the investor change the interest rate from 9.9% to 5.5%, the maximum allowed in September 2014, when the loan was written. They also asked that the investor return the overpayment of money by the borrowers during the time since the investor purchased the note. The difference between the loan at 9.9% (payment of $370.18) and 5.5% (payment of 241.54) for the period that the investor owned the note (40 months) would be $5,145.60. The investor now had to pay this amount back to the borrower. The investor had to pay the legal costs for the note and mortgage to be drawn, executed, and recorded.

The moral of the story here is that during the due diligence process, there is a need to examine all the paperwork to ensure compliance with all legal requirements. Although the investor did this, he was unaware of usury laws in Pennsylvania limiting the interest rate. Had they known this, he could have negotiated a lower price from the note seller since it was out of legal compliance. When you are new to note investing, knowing what to look for during due diligence is critical. This is another reason new investors should consider partnering with an experienced investor through partial purchases or hypothecation.

Case Study #4: Georgia

This is an excellent example of a fairly easy-performing note on a property located in Georgia. I purchased this in November of 2019 for $30,985. The unpaid balance was $38,730. The principal and interest payment for this loan is $351.03. This borrower pays on time every month and is occasionally late by a week or so, but they pay the $17.55 late fee. As with the other notes, a servicing company handles everything for me, so I mainly see the e-mail notifying me that I got money deposited in my account.

Since this note had a substantial discount, I expected significant issues. During my due diligence, I determined that the borrower most likely ran into an interruption in employment. Once that was resolved, payments were more regular. They had been irregular for a time, sometimes being as late as 60 days. Since I purchased the note, this borrower has not been more than 20 days late maximum. And when they are more than 14 days late, they pay with the late payment included. The other thing that scared people off and created the discount was that this was a manufactured home. Before purchasing the note, I confirmed they had a "Certificate of Permanent Location," which verifies that the borrower also owns the real estate upon which the home sits, making it part of the real property for legal purposes, including foreclosure. This is a crucial detail to look for if you are lending on a manufactured home.

The Numbers:

- Note Price: $30,985
- Unpaid balance: $38,730
- Note discounted 20.2%
- Note rate: 10%
- Yield (since I purchased at a discount):12.89%
- Property Value: $89,000
- Loan to Value Ratio: 65%

Case Study #5: North Carolina Note Expo Award-Winning Deal

In February 2019, I purchased a note on the property in North Carolina for $30,015. The unpaid balance was $33,702.66, with an interest rate of 10.04%. With 120 months left on the note, I had a yield of 12.48%. In June 2019, I sold a partial of this note to another investor. He purchased 96 months of the note for $32,000, which gave him a 7.18% interest rate. Everything was fine until the servicing company received a hardship letter in July 2020.

The borrower was an 80-year-old lady who cleaned houses to supplement her Social Security income. This helped her cover her expenses, including her loan payment. Due to COVID, she could no longer clean houses and lost that extra income. She was distraught that she would lose her home. My partial investor told me he did not want to deal with any of this, even though I told him I would handle things. I purchased the note back from him to smooth things out for him. (He reinvested with me, but with hypothecation, since it was much easier for him.)

Working with the servicing company, I received authorization to speak with her directly to see what could be done. She had become very attached to this home after many years, and the thought of leaving frightened her. I told her I was very good at numbers and budgets and that we could figure something out. We reviewed her entire budget, and I devised a way for her to stay in the house. She was adamant about not wanting charity, so I told her she would make a house payment- I would just be restructuring the loan. Because I purchased this note at a discount, I was able to lower her unpaid balance, and I lowered her interest rate. I also made this an interest-only loan. I do not recommend purchasing interest-only loans for various reasons, but because this lady was in her 80s already, I did not think this would be a long-term note. Due to legal requirements, we had to make a balloon payment in 10 years. This means she would pay interest only for ten years, and then she would have to pay off the entire balance. She was very concerned, but I told her we would do a new note before the unpaid balance was due. She was happy with this arrangement.

The Numbers:

- Original note: Unpaid balance $33,702.66
- Note Price: $30,015
- Note Rate: 10.04%
- Yield: 12.48%
- Property Value: $68,000
- Loan to Value Ratio: 50.5%
- Loan Modification:
- New Unpaid Balance: $30,658
- Interest Rate: 7.5%
- Interest Only Payment: $191.61
- Balloon Payment in 2030

She was very grateful to stay in the house and had the continued dignity of making her monthly Loan payment for her home. She paid on time every month until September 2023, when I got a notice that she passed away. The following month, her estate paid off the note. I cannot say this was my most lucrative deal, but I did get a return on my investment, and I could keep an 80-year-old lady from losing her house.

Final Thoughts:

Note investing is not merely about buying and selling notes; it's about understanding the intricacies of the market, recognizing opportunities, and managing risks effectively. The knowledge and insights in this book are designed to equip you with the tools needed to navigate the complex landscape of note investing confidently.

As you venture into note investing, remember that continuous learning and adaptation are crucial. The market is dynamic, and staying informed about the latest trends, regulations, and best practices will help you maintain a competitive edge.

Note investing offers a unique blend of risk and reward, combining elements of real estate investment with the financial intricacies of lending. It provides a pathway to diversify your investment portfolio, generate passive income, and achieve long-term financial goals.

As you move forward, remember the core tenets of successful investing: patience, diligence, and continuous improvement. The journey of note investing is not without its challenges, but it can be gratifying with the proper knowledge and approach.

Thank you for embarking on this journey with me. This book has provided you with valuable insights and practical guidance to help you succeed in the world of note investing. Here's to your future success and the profitable investments that lie ahead!

CHAPTER 15

About the Author

Dave Storton has over two decades of business experience. He founded DSRT Property Solutions, LLC in 2016 after retiring from the San Jose Police Department as Detective Commander of the Financial Crimes Unit. During his career, Dave received two hazardous duty medals and the Blue and Gold Wounded in Service award. He also worked with the state of California to infuse leadership, ethics, and community policing into the police Academy curriculum used in every Academy in California. He is a three-time award-winning investor recognized at Note Expo by leaders in the note investment space. He is a founding member of The Seller Finance Coalition. DSRT invests private capital in real estate notes and other real estate investments, providing solid returns for investors who partner with Dave.

DSRT Property Solutions, LLC
Contact Dave:
Dave@DSRT.us
www.dsrt.us

www.ingramcontent.com/pod-product-compliance
Lightning Source LLC
Chambersburg PA
CBHW071232210326
41597CB00016B/2017